GROOVE ESSENTIALS 2.0

THE GROOVE ENCYCLOPEDIA FOR THE ADVANCED 21ST-CENTURY DRUMMER

TOMMY IGOE ▪ VIC FIRTH ▪ HUDSON MUSIC

GROOVE ESSENTIALS 2.0

Written by Tommy Igoe

Design—Jo Hay

Editing—Joe Bergamini

Notation Engraving—Jack Mansager

Basses—Vashon Johnson

Guitars—Kevin Kuhn

Keyboards—Ted Baker

Piano—Allen Farnham

Percussion—Rolando Morales-Matos

Additional Keyboards and Percussion —Tommy Igoe

All songs written by Kevin Kuhn, Ted Baker, Vashon Johnson, Allen Farnham and Tommy Igoe
except "An Orchestral Experience for Drummers" arranged by Tommy Igoe

All songs © 2008 Deep Rhythm Music

Recorded, Produced, Mixed and Mastered by Tommy Igoe.

Tommy Igoe exclusively plays: Vic Firth Sticks, Mallets and Brushes, Drum Workshop Drums,
Zildjian Cymbals, Evans Drumheads, Latin Percussion and Rhythm Tech.

ISBN: 1423464451
HL6620125

www.hudsonmusic.com
©℗ 2008 Hudson Music, LLC

About the Disc

Groove Essentials was the world's first educational package to feature audio using an MP3 disc, which allowed us to fit the equivalent of five audio CDs onto one disc. Since it's debut, many other products have followed our lead, which makes my geeky-techno-junkie side proud.

iPods (or any brand of MP3 player) have been a revolutionary practice tool for musicians. Having all your material right there in one unit with the ability to quickly locate and manipulate each track is an amazing convenience. The *GE* disc is designed for you to get this music into your computer easily and quickly so you can then use it with your portable music player or, if you wish, convert the tracks into Audio CDs. 99% of the over 50,000 users (at the time of this writing) had no problem using the disc, but a few people needed extra help. With this page, I'm confident we'll get everyone up and running with no problems.

HERE IS WHAT YOU NEED TO KNOW AND WHAT YOU HAVE TO DO. IT'S EASY.

- The included disc is an MP3 formatted data disc. It is **not** an "audio CD" and therefore it will **not** play in plain old vanilla CD players. It will only play in CD players that are "MP3 Disc Capable." If you aren't sure if your CD player has this functionality, simply insert the disc and see if it plays.

- Open your music library program on your computer (I use iTunes, but you can use any flavor of program you wish, as well as Windows or Macintosh). Your main music library screen should be showing. You should also have the following parameters showing: Title, Artist, Album and Beats per Minute (BPM).

- Insert the *GE* disc into your machine, and the disc icon should appear on your desktop.

- Simply drag the disc icon onto your main library screen. From this point, all the tracks should automatically import without you having to do anything at all. If you have problems, you may need to double click the disc (where all the tracks should appear in a list) and drag the tracks over as a group or individually.

- You may also wish to select "Import" from the "File" menu and select the tracks from that screen. No matter which method you use, just get those tracks imported into your library. All the tracks will be automatically labeled with the correct Title (Groove #), Artist (Tommy Igoe), Album (*Groove Essentials* 2.0) and BPM of each track, so you don't have to do a thing. Nice, right?

- That's all you have to do to get up and running! At this point, you may transfer them to your iPod or burn them to audio CDs from within iTunes. Remember that the disc is a data disc that we had to trick into listing the files in the correct order. There are two "dummy" letters in front of each track that you can either ignore or remove; your choice. So the track listed on the disc as "ia 48-slow", is simply "Groove 48 slow" in the book.

For those into recording, all the tracks in GE 2.0 were recorded using an 8-core Mac Pro with Logic Studio , Apogee converters, Presonus Mic Preamps and DI's, Neumann and Sennheiser Microphones, Waves SSL, V-Series and API Plug-Ins and then converted to MP3 files using the highest quality codecs and rates possible.

Introduction

Welcome to Groove Essentials 2.0
In this book, you will experience the following:

- *Enjoyment*
- *Satisfaction*
- *Thrills*
- *Pride*
- *Hope*
- *Self-respect*
- *Warmth*
- *Happiness*
- *Fun*
- *Contentment*
- *Exhilaration*
- *Delight*
- *Laughter*
- *Love*—like sending me e-mails about how life before *Groove Essentials* was boring, dull, and meaningless.

Some other things you will experience:

- *Frustration*
- *Anger*
- *Disillusionment*
- *Aggravation*
- *Annoyance*
- *Disappointment*
- *Swearing (G- or X-rated, your choice)*
- *Hopelessness*
- *Disenchantment*
- *Self-Loathing*
- *Self-Ridicule ("nice fill, idiot!")*
- *Violence—as in wanting to hurl your drums off a cliff*
- *Hate—as in sending me e-mails about how Groove Essentials is toxic and I am the evil spawn of Satan. (It's okay, I know it's not personal...)*

Everyone will experience all of these things in different ways and in different combinations. But regardless of talent level, aspirations and experience, you must have one crucially important quality within you to have success with this book:

PERSEVERANCE

Perseverance is defined as "the determined continuation with something." I like that. "Determined continuation": Are there any more important words in exploring an art form? Are there any more important words in *anything* worth exploring? From climbing a mountain to studying to be a doctor, is there anything more important in your quest for knowledge than making a commitment to perseverance? I mention this because you'll need it for what's in store.

When Things Get Tough...

It's the hard days—those steep hills—that will test your commitment to the instrument. On the days where you can't do anything right (and those days are inevitable), you may be tempted to give it all up. Watching TV, playing video games, checking e-mail, eating; *anything* will sound more appetizing than playing drums on those tough days. But while short breaks are good, never let a few bad days destroy your love for drumming. And remember that musical progress isn't linear. You will have magical days followed by times of bewildering ineptness, which is completely normal.

GE 2.0 is not an exercise book. It is designed to be as close as possible to a real-life musical experience, without the actual musicians being in the room with you. Therefore, you simply cannot use a vanilla, "play-this-pattern-with-a-click-and-then-move-to-the-next-pattern" mentality. You must be an interactive partner; a player who breathes, sweats, and has an opinion on what to do at certain musical moments. I want you to get your hands dirty with this music. Get in there and wrestle around, and yes, take a few punches, too. Get a black eye, a bloody nose. It's fun! Clean up and do it again. When you fail, you learn. What happened? Why? Fix it. Get back in there. Better? Thought so. Set 'em up and knock 'em down, baby.

When Things Go Right...

Man, there is nothing better than those "perfect" days of drumming, right? If only you could bottle that feeling. You know the ones (or you soon will), where you can't do anything wrong: every groove, every fill, every solo is so flawless you can actually feel their perfection in your soul. Oh, to feel like that all the time! Well, it would be nice, but you can't.

Hey, what gives? You're supposed to be all rah-rah, saying "you can do anything you put your mind to, slugger!" Sorry, I can't lie to you. If it were that simple to *think* your way to musical greatness, we'd all be amazing drummers. Highs and lows are an infuriating, though normal part of the musical journey. However, it's easy to ride out those peaks and valleys with this simple nugget:

"You're never as bad as you feel on your worst day and you're never as good as you feel on your best."

(You know, Tommy, if this whole drumming thing doesn't work out, you could write fortune cookies for a living—Hudson Music.)

Thank you gents, great advice. But seriously, that's all you need to know to keep things in perspective. Great days are no more a true barometer of your talent than the days where you can't do anything right. Don't get cocky and don't get depressed. I've seen too many players get their heads all screwed-up because they couldn't deal with the emotional rollercoaster that inevitably comes with exploring an artform.

You know, these aren't simple daily changes either. Sometimes, these wild variances in your perceived abilities can last months or years! Long swoops of joy and misery are common. We *all* experience them, but I believe the successful among us ride them out with a positive, "glass half-full" mentality, knowing the lows are temporary and that better music is around the corner. "Positive Realism" is my musical motto, and it has served me well. I hope it does for you, too.

So, make a promise to yourself right now that no matter what *GE 2.0* throws your way, you'll keep your head up and your eyes looking forward to the great results that all your hard work will bring.

DRUMMER, KNOW THYSELF

GE is designed to push you into confronting your musical weaknesses. The basics of surviving real musical situations behind the drumset are frighteningly simple. Ready?
- ■ *Time (Groove)*
- ■ *Fills (Solos)*
- ■ *Musicality (concept, balance, phrasing, delivery, and all the other intangibles that define your sound and musical contribution).*

And that, folks, is that. Everything distilled down to three little points. You know, small lists are scarier than big ones. Big ones, well, it's easy to get lost in the sea of *blah, blah, blah.* But little ones? You've got nowhere to run. *GE* will gently—and with *GE 2.0,* not so gently—point out where you've got work to do. But the moral of the story is we've *all* got work to do, every one of us, on every level. The work, when it comes to exploring an art form, never, ever stops for anybody.

Train Your Ears—Free Your Mind

Like rudiments can free your hands (if taught properly), *GE* is here to free your mind. I know that may sound a bit existential, but that's not where I'm coming from. I'm all about practical application and practical education on the drums, so it makes sense this book is rooted in a practical philosophy.

Groove Essentials, more than anything else, is ear training for the drums. There is no more important concept that I'll be able to show you than training your ears to hear yourself honestly and react quickly to musical events. *Hearing* that perfect groove, *hearing* that tasty fill, *hearing* the manipulation of ghost notes that affect the pocket of a groove—this is the good stuff! Once you get past simply playing the grooves, you can really manipulate the music if you can *hear* your drumming honestly. And, most importantly, by working with all these great pieces of music, you'll be training your ears to appreciate and react to other instruments with grace and sensitivity. You won't be playing the drums for yourself; you'll be playing for the band.

So, one more time for those who missed it in the original *GE* (because I said it so many times that it became sort of a running gag): record yourself! RECORD YOURSELF, RECORD YOURSELF, RECORD YOURSELF, RECORD YOURSELF. RECORD YOURSELF!!! And when you are finished, RECORD YOURSELF AGAIN! (Am I being too subtle?) To train your ears, you simply must record yourself because only on playback, away from the physical toil of performance, can you hear your musical contribution as it really is. And now, in the 21st century, it's easier and cheaper than ever to get some kind of recording solution in your practice space so you can listen back to your performance. And it's getting easier all the time. No excuses.

Be A Groove Architect

Where the original *GE* DVD focused on the "connective tissue" of grooves—the stuff that binds grooves together—*GE 2.0* focuses on a more advanced topic for our ears: "Groove Construction." Each and every groove offered here utilizes something unique in terms of groove design. Groove addition, groove subtraction, rhythmic manipulation, motivic transference, tempo dependency, rideless construction, and implied modulations are a few of the techniques discussed on the DVD, and now you will get to explore them with these tracks.

The idea with groove construction is to gain awareness of the things that make grooves unique. Even though some grooves may look similar, the simplest shift of a bass drum note can affect the overall symmetry and appropriate application. Analyzing and understanding groove construction is one of the most powerful tools to raise you from the simple "player of beat" to the level of a groove architect. An architect is a creator, and you want to be an architect of grooves. Not a regurgitator of what's been done before, but a skilled craftsman who is free to interact with musicians and contribute to the overall artistic statement.

And this would be a good time to remind those of, shall we say, an "adventurous spirit" that practicing on the gig is the best way to lose a gig. We're going to add a ton of new stuff to our musical toolbox in *GE 2.0,* but, as always, it's your job to use those tools with sensitivity. Call me old-fashioned, but if you've got a wedding gig tomorrow, I don't think I'd try some motivic transference on a rousing rendition of "Hot, Hot, Hot." Just practice at home and try out new stuff in rehearsals. There are piles of discarded drummer carcasses who simply couldn't obey that simple philosophy.

Make Musical Decisions

The first thing that freaks out my students is when they hear me scream, "Don't just do what I did on the DVD!" Here's the deal with my performances on the DVD: They are just one version on one day. They work, they sound good, they are fine demonstrations of hearing what the groove sounds like with real music. Which is exactly what they are supposed to be. Nothing more, nothing less.

But, the play-along is so much more than that! These are the full-length versions of the songs we created for the grooves. That means there are multiple parts and various instrument combinations for you to experiment with. So when the bass cuts out at letter B, or you have to groove with the percussion alone at letter D, you have to make *musical decisions!* You can't simply plug the main groove in, play it for 3 minutes, and call that a satisfying musical experience. That's why this book is so great to use with a good teacher. You and your teacher can discuss options and try out different ideas of how to approach each piece of music. An hour will go by in what seems like 2 minutes when you have lessons like that, trust me.

What you see me playing on the DVD roughly corresponds to the last time through the form of the play-along songs. I'm usually playing pretty hard and strong since the entire band is in at that point. Just keep that in mind for when you hear the other sections of the songs in the play-along (especially the beginnings). You have to make a lot of decisions. And that's the fun!

You also have a lot of fill and soloing opportunities too. By all means, you can play some of the fills I play on the DVD, but do your own thing, too. You have to play BAD fills to know what GOOD fills sound like. So just let your imagination run wild and experiment freely in the privacy of your practice room (door's closed, right?). For the longer solo opportunities in this book, you can push your musical boundaries. There are solos over vamps, ensemble hits, long forms, short repeats, and more. If you are weak at soloing, that's okay (this is *Groove Essentials* after all), my advice is to first groove through the solo space to acquaint yourself with playing alone at the appropriate time. From there, you can start to spread your wings at your own pace. Do not be afraid to copy solo ideas from your drum heroes.

The Charts

Just as with the original book, the charts are underwritten with deliberate notational inconsistencies like you'd see in real life. They offer almost no help, and have very little in the way of figures—just enough for you to play what you have to play, but not nearly enough for you to play everything you should play. Most writers are expecting the drummer, as the legendary arranger Don Sebesky puts it, "to have the expertise to know what to do." So, they'll give you a little cue here, a little ensemble figure there, and a whole lot of slashes.

And that is all you need. You already know my position on the many books written touting "professional charts!" and how they are simply over-notated ink-fests that have nothing to do with professional playing. Oh, yes, you may once in a blue moon see a chart that looks like the legendary "Black Page," but those times are rare, and usually the music is dense and in need of large amounts of rehearsal for the entire band anyway, so you'll have some time to figure it out. Don't worry if you can't read (though you must learn if you are a serious student of the instrument), because 95 percent of reading charts is counting bars and being aware of where you are. And you don't have to be a great reader (or even read at all) to count bars and feel "8 bars" and then another "6 bars" or whatever. Everyone can count. This isn't hard and you *can* do it.

Get Your Groove On

Here we go: Same format, same construction, same "click-less" tracks as the original—a mind-bending 53 brand-new grooves to complete the *Groove Essentials* repertoire. Let me just say this one last time (I say it on the DVD, too): I am assuming you have already worked through the original book. An understanding of the first 47 grooves, and the multitude of concepts that went along with them, are essential to getting the most out of this more-advanced material. I'm not going to repeat any of the information from the first book here, like how to read the charts, what the various symbols mean, or even what "clave" is. We did all that. And I know I can't stop you from starting here, but you'll be doing yourself a big musical favor by completing the original book and DVD before you tackle this beast. There, I said my piece. Now do what you want…

Lastly, thank you all, sincerely, for the amazing enthusiasm that was shown and the incredible feedback you gave me to create *GE 2.0*. I truly could not have done it without you. I set a link on my website to take suggestions for grooves that people wanted to see, and I received over 3000 e-mails! The publishers and I were blown away. Everyone had a voice, and the Bo Diddley and the Train beat are included because of the overwhelming votes they received. And that's a great thing: those are classic and important grooves, and I don't know if I would have included them or not without your voice, so thank you for helping steer the vision of *GE 2.0*. I'm confident it's a stronger educational package with your input. And to those whose suggestion doesn't appear, I apologize. Your voice was heard but tough decisions had to be made. As you'll see, I carefully designed *GE 2.0* so each groove would have a unique *groove construction* element that will expand your overall musicianship.

So, remember our favorite word: Perseverance. If you feel lost or hopeless, stop and take a deep breath. Collect your thoughts, calm your musical mind, and try again. If you feel great, you owe it to yourself to record it. Get out that musical microscope and analyze your drumming. There are years of study waiting within these pages, and it took me decades to master all these genres (and I'm still not done), so take your time. And, above all else, even on those tough days, always, always, always…

ENJOY THE JOURNEY!

P.S. Literally, the day before we shipped this book off to the printer, we lost one of the true titans our instrument, a man whose groove graced thousands of recordings, the legendary Earl Palmer. I'd like to dedicate GE 2.0 *to his incredible legacy. Heaven's band just got a lot more funky.*

Chapter 1
ROCK Grooves

Groove 48 SLOW Track 01

Variation A

Variation B

CHART

BOOGALOO ROCK

Groove 48 Slow and Fast were designed specifically for you to analyze your ghost- and grace-note control. As I demonstrated on the DVD, ghost notes are soft notes that have rhythmic value and grace notes are soft notes that do NOT have rhythmic value. They are powerful tools to put your own unique stamp on any groove that comes your way.

Be aware that *all* instruments can play ghost and grace notes, not just drummers. In fact, listen closely to the tracks and you'll hear all the musicians employing ghost and grace notes in everything they play. That's what gives good rhythm-section playing its nuance. On this boogaloo-type groove, you can record your performance and analyze your control of these crucially important groove modifiers.

Groove 48 FAST Track 02

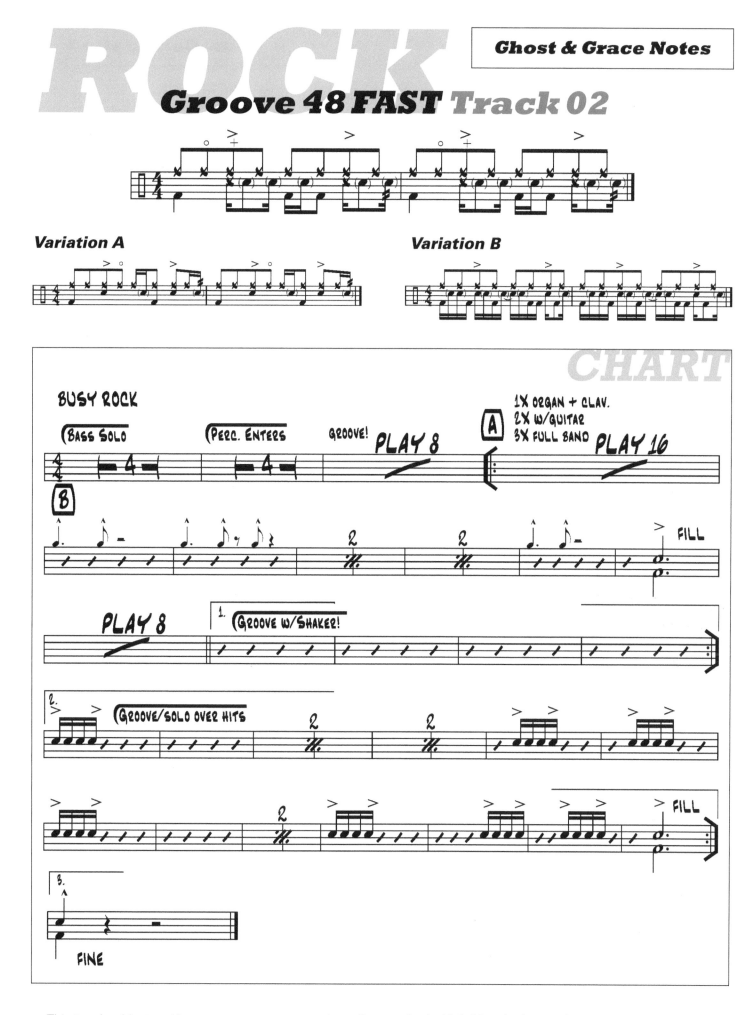

Variation A

Variation B

CHART

BUSY ROCK

(BASS SOLO   (PERC. ENTERS   GROOVE!   PLAY 8

1X ORGAN + CLAV.
2X W/GUITAR
3X FULL BAND   PLAY 16

PLAY 8   1. (GROOVE W/SHAKER!

2. (GROOVE/SOLO OVER HITS

FILL

FINE

This tune's a blast and is at a great tempo to get into all sorts of mischief. After the bass solo at the top, come right in with that groove smooth as silk. Check out variation B, which will sound terrible if you play it loud. Keep it crisp. Watch that tricky solo! One wrong move and it's all over.

ROCK

Groove 49 Track 03

Variation A

Variation B

CHART

SLOW ROCK BALLAD
(1 BAR COUNT-OFF)

1X TRIO W/SHAKER
2X SHAKER OUT
3X W/GUITAR (CRESC. INTO Ⓐ)

PLAY 3X

(4)

FILL

Ⓐ

(4)

FILL

1.

2. SOLO

3.

FINE

One of the toughest songs in this book is right here, folks. Really slow rock ballads can rush or drag like crazy if you aren't completely committed to the tempo. Here, you get to experience just how much control you have over a very slow rock ballad. The fill you play before the sixteenth figure is only 2½ beats long but can seem like it takes forever and, of course, there is no click—don't be angry; it's because I care. Variation B, which I play on the DVD, is a nod of respect to an excellent songwriter and underappreciated drummer, Phil Collins.

ROCK

Groove 50 Track 04

Variation A

Variation B

We're always adding! Here is a simple example of "groove subtraction:" a fantastic technique to create new textures and feels. We're taking out beat 2 from the usual backbeat slot, so we'll only have a backbeat on beat four. Try playing this tune with a "regular" rock beat and see how different it feels and sounds. The difference is incredible! Variations A and B both show how you can accessorize the first beat for a bit more rhythmic motion.

Groove 51 SLOW Track 05

Variation A

Variation B

Let's flip "four on the floor" on its head and put it on the snare. Now, you already know how I don't like "brand names" assigned to grooves—it locks in your thinking—but just be aware this is sometimes referred to as the "Motown" beat. Ugh. *Rant: Motown is much too diverse to be distilled into one little beat!* Variation B uses ghosted syncopations on the bass drum, but if you play them loud, it sounds terrible.

Groove 51 FAST Track 06

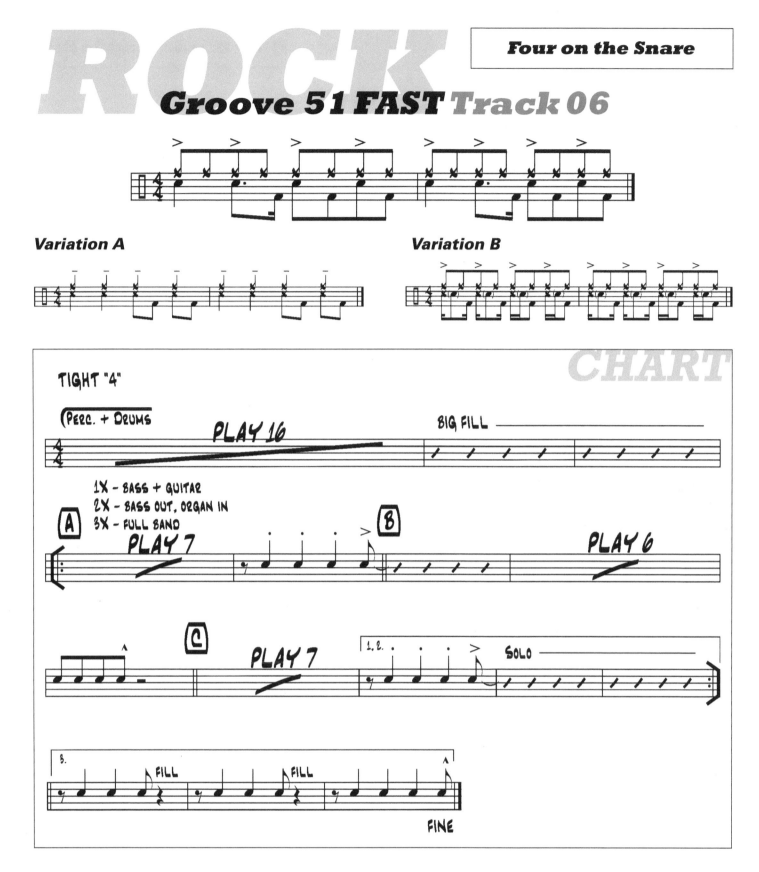

Hang on, baby; there's some notes flying around on this one. Vashon is going off on the bass, Kevin's laying down some of that Philly Phunk guitar (he is from Philly, you know), and what is your job supposed to be? You are the center, the sole unifying force for all of the rhythmic madness going on in the rhythm section. Jeez, no pressure, right? Those four quarter notes on the snare have to be perfect because the band will be listening to them to get their bearings on where to place their stuff. Just like they'd be listening to a click if you were in a studio environment, they are listening to you on a real gig. *You are the click.* Variation A uses a sloshy hi-hat, a great way to change the flavor of the drumset overall. Variation B uses the tricky, yet great "soft-ghost-after-rimshot" technique. Hard to play, but worth the effort.

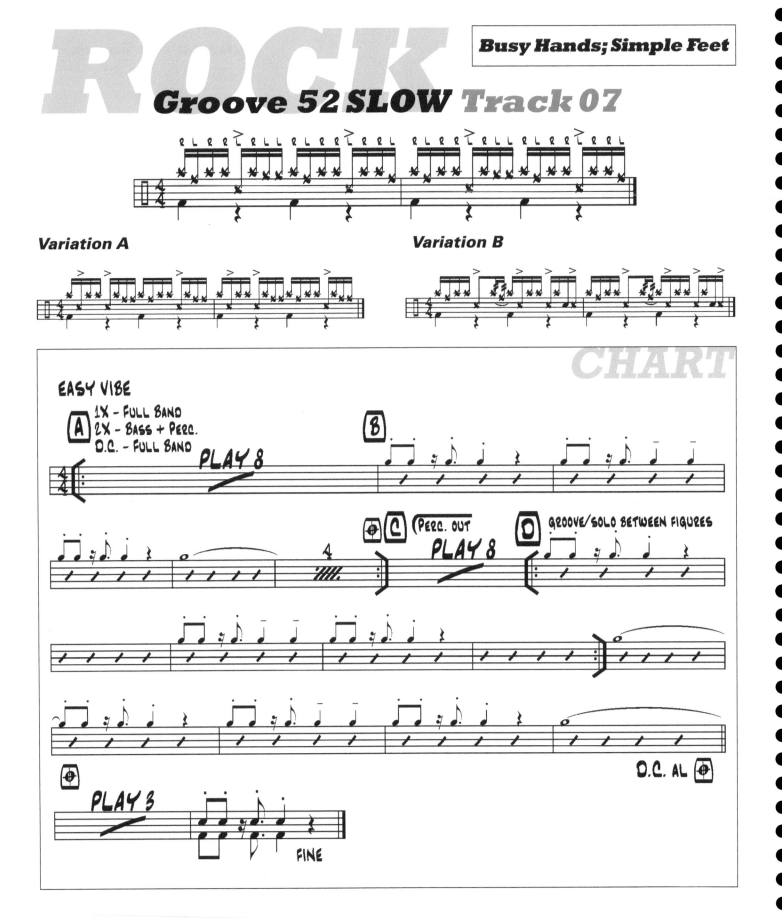

Variation A

Variation B

Here's a groove featuring a nice stream of sixteenths, using two different sound sources, while the bass drum simply lays out 1 and 3. Busy hands, simple feet: a great groove-construction technique. But for goodness sake, don't *think* paradiddles—you'll groove about as hard as a newborn kitten. This is why you do all that rudimental work, so your hands just go by themselves on grooves like this. This song is our tribute to the late, great Grover Washington. Listen to his legendary records and the incredible musicians who played on them.

ROCK

Groove 52 FAST Track 08

Variation A

Variation B

Besides working on the obvious drum stuff with this fast and dense song, the beginning also focuses on a common weakness that drummers without formal training run into: counting rests. I'm going to bring this important concept up again throughout the book, but here's a great chance to practice counting 32 bars of rest at the top. The synth strings are all over the place (as orchestral parts can often be), so listen to the click and concentrate! There is no room for error, because your big solo kicks the band into the groove. Imagine what would happen if you were one bar off. The entire thing would come crashing to a halt and you'd have to suffer the glaring stares of the entire orchestra. Not fun. The point is that counting rests is a big musical responsibility. Variations A and B feature a slick right-hand motion on the ride utilizing a bell accent.

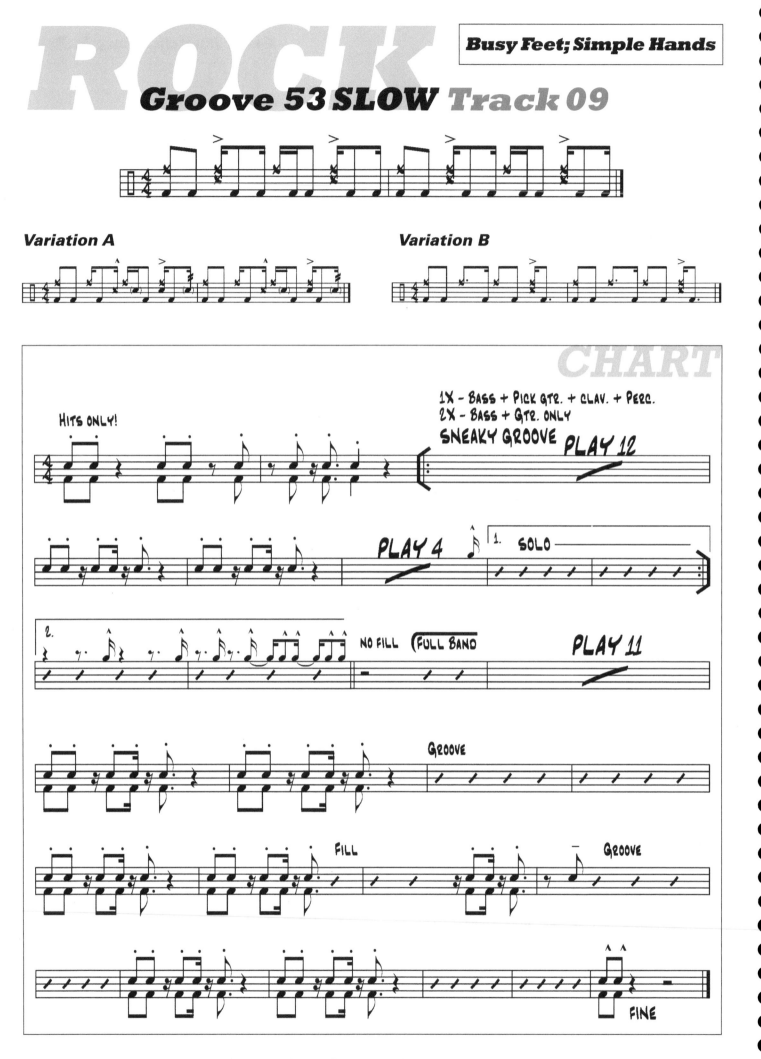

Variation A

Variation B

Busy bass drum combined with simple hands: another great technique.

GROOVE ESSENTIALS 2.0

Groove 53 FAST Track 10

Variation A

Variation B

CHART

"INTRO"
NO GROOVE - FLOAT

3X CYMS - - - - - - - - -

FILL

A GROOVE!
PLAY 8

BRIDGE
PLAY 4

PLAY 3

1.
PLAY 3

SOLO

2.
PLAY 3

3.
PLAY 3

FILL

FILL

FINE

This song is such blast to play. You are going to have limitless options to explore your creativity here, while still serving the groove. Check out how the musicians are phrasing their parts with different interpretations. It's a great sound, but man, the drums on songs like this really bring it altogether. Also note the beginning, where it tells you to "float." Compared to the original *GE*, these songs are more sophisticated, and this concept of "floating" is going to come up again and again. You need to create a feeling of implied rhythm but without a full groove attached to it. Listening Hands the sound of the music at these moments is the key to how you'll create your part.

Variations A and B give you different options for creating a busy groove but with different orchestration concepts. Try them all and then make up your own.

Groove 54 SLOW Track 11

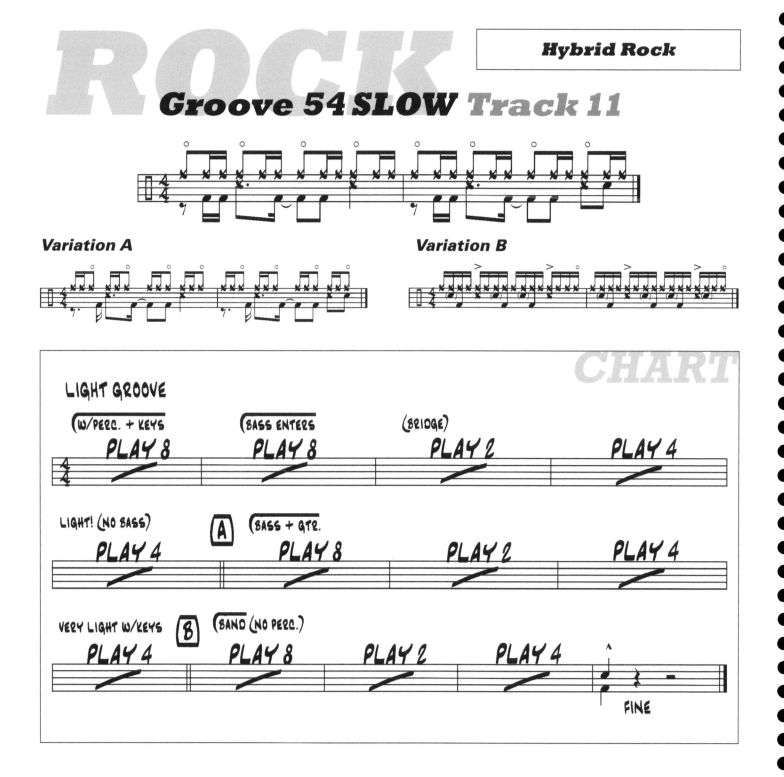

Variation A

Variation B

CHART

LIGHT GROOVE

(W/ PERC. + KEYS	(BASS ENTERS	(BRIDGE)	
PLAY 8	PLAY 8	PLAY 2	PLAY 4

LIGHT! (NO BASS)	A (BASS + GTR.		
PLAY 4	PLAY 8	PLAY 2	PLAY 4

VERY LIGHT W/KEYS B	(BAND (NO PERC.)			
PLAY 4	PLAY 8	PLAY 2	PLAY 4	FINE

When I play a recording of this groove for students while plopping a paper and pencil down in front of them, I often get a scrawling mural that resembles a Rorschach test more than a groove transcription. And it's not hard to understand why...

This groove, to those who are not used to this incredibly useful hi-hat part, can be hard to figure out and even stranger to play. There is a lot of stuff going on, especially for a "rock" groove (whatever that means in the 21st century). But that's the idea. The walls are falling down more and more all the time, and the era of thinking that rock grooves are simplistic, easy-to-play banging is long gone. This rock groove borrows from R&B, and you can even see the similarity of the hi-hat part to a jazz ride beat. No, you jazz purists out there, it isn't the same. It's just similar, so take it easy. This is a hybrid rock groove that borrows from other genres to create a sophisticated groove that you'll have a great time getting used to. Grooves like this could just as easily be at home in the World or R&B sections—another reason I don't subscribe to labels very often. Variation A reverses the hi-hat part (what a difference!), and B changes the hi-hat to running sixteenths with a fast open/close on the end of the bar.

Groove 54 FAST Track 12

Variation A

Variation B

CHART

GROOVE W/PERC + BASS

PLAY 8   PLAY 7   (PERC. FILL   PLAY 8

GROOVE/SOLO W/PERC.

A (+ PIANO

PLAY 4   PLAY 8   PLAY 7   FILL

PLAY 8   SOLO

B (FULL BAND

PLAY 8   PLAY 7   (GTR. BREAK   PLAY 8

PLAY 4

FINE

Just try to play this groove hard and heavy, and you'll wind up tired and defeated. Light hnd crisp will keep it tight and in the pocket. "Light" doesn't mean soft or weak. Rather, it's playing with snap and a quick stick velocity to make the drums pop and crack. Variations A and B both create a different flavor by manipulation of the hi-hat part.

ROCK

Groove 55 Track 13

Variation A

Variation B

CHART

LIGHT GROOVE

8X

A (B.B. ON "3" PLAY 12

mf

4X (PIANO ONLY AD-LIB CYMBALS

p p

B GROOVE PLAY 12 LIGHT! PLAY 16

mf

C (W/LEAD GTR. PLAY 12 PLAY 8

f mp FINE

Let's take a look at three rock waltzes and see how tiny changes in each have huge impacts on the songs they apply to. This groove has a backbeat (B.B.) on beat 3, which makes it entirely contained in one bar. It's so easy to take a groove like this for granted. I mean, look at it! You're right, it doesn't look like anything special; however, it's these taken-for-granted grooves that separate the good and great groove players. If you simply play it like it looks, it'll just sit there like a fat dog. It's all on your *delivery*. Note how variation A uses foot splashes to create a some length inside the groove. Don't use this groove the entire song; just drop it in once in a while as a spice. Legatos and staccatos are incredible groove construction tools. Use them!

GROOVE ESSENTIALS 2.0

Groove 56 Track 14

Variation A

Variation B

Now the backbeat is on beat 1, which makes the groove six beats long, and boy, doesn't that just change everything. Notice anything else about the track compared to Groove 55? This tempo is significantly faster and is based on quarter notes instead of eighths. Groove construction, right? This piece was written as a tribute to Spinal Tap, one of the best bands ever, and I think Kevin played the awesome guitar solo behind his head. Please, do not spontaneously combust.

ROCK

Rock Waltz (Shuffled)

Variation A

Variation B

CHART

SHUFFLE ROCK WALTZ

PLAY 14

PLAY 6

PLAY 16

A (GTR. OUT!)

PLAY 16

PLAY 6

PLAY 16

FILL

(FULL BAND)

PLAY 16

PLAY 6

PLAY 8

PLAY 8

FINE

Whenever you swing or "shuffle" something, it naturally encourages active ghost and grace notes because of the circular construction of triplets. Allow your drumming to explore this wonderful groove characteristic. This is one of my favorite tracks to play; the band is so gloriously loose! Loose is different from sloppy. In our sterile, quantized world, don't lose the ability to appreciate organic grooves with a lot of human phrasing.

Variation A

Variation B

CHART

50's STYLE GROOVE

ETC... PLAY 7

PLAY 7 FILL [A] (PIANO OUT PLAY 8

PLAY 7 FILL [B] (GTR. IN PLAY 8

PLAY 7

FINE

I try to throw a little history into each *Groove Essentials* release, and here we're going back to play a classic slow 12/8 in a 1950s Doo-Wop style. The coolest thing about the '50s rock era was how varied the rhythm sections played. Listen to some tracks back to back and you'll hear everything from a tight swing to perfectly straight eighths and lots of the un-writable stuff in between. This simple 12/8 groove was the rhythmic "bed" for many hits, including songs like "Earth Angel" by the Penguins.

Variation A adds a little hi-hat open/close action and variation B explores one possibility for adding grace notes before the downbeat. Remember, with this type of grace notes, the sound you want to make is "shoop," with a very soft "sh" sound. If the drums sound like "bzzap!," then work a bit on those soft little grace notes to get them soft and smooth.

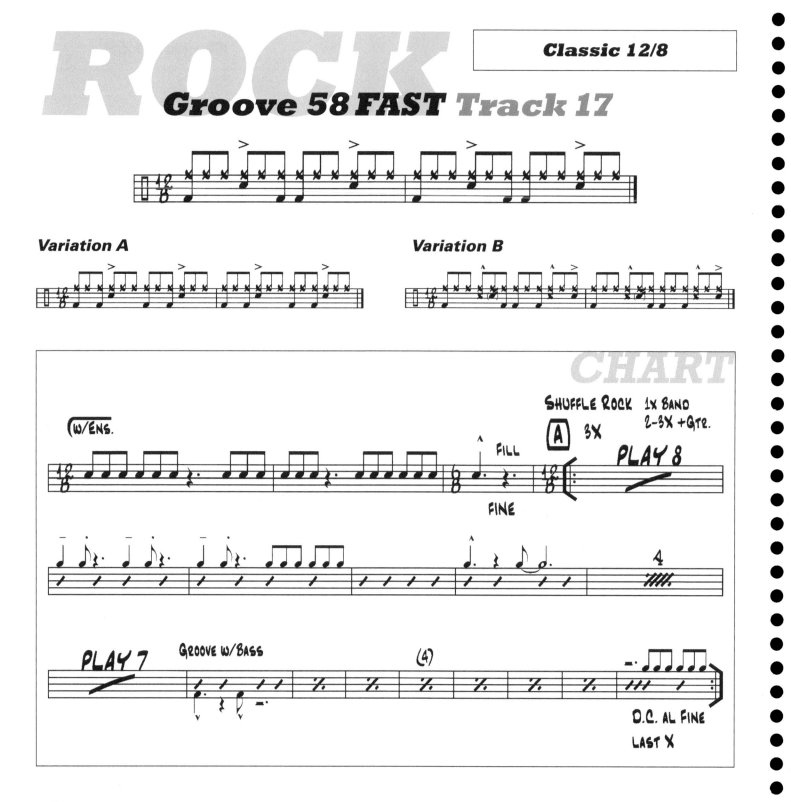

Variation A

Variation B

Fascinating how this simple groove can propel such completely different pieces of music, isn't it? The Doo-Wop thing is way, way behind us now, and you'll have to really up your game to drive this song.

With a solid approach to playing this groove, you give the other musicians license to sit back in the pocket, creating that magic that can only occur with living, breathing human beings playing music. Remember the old bug-a-boo about playing faster: you'll naturally want to play harder. No, no, no! You are all so much smarter than that because you went through the original *GE*, right? Right!

The 12/8 rock groove often splits into groups of three naturally, which is fine, but try not to accent the hi-hat too much. It should flow through the groove while the kick and snare take care of the accenting. Over-accented hi-hat parts will clutter up a groove and make it sluggish. A sensitive touch is so important.

Variation B looks tough, with the grace notes after the rim shot, but it's not that bad. The trick is the keep the stick down after the backbeat and letting it press along the head leading directly to the bass drum note. It's a fantastic sound.

Groove 59 SLOW Track 18

Variation A

Variation B

Just by moving one little note—one little note is all it takes!—we have something different, useful, and new. We simply moved the bass drum note off of beat 3 and put it on the last note of the triplet. That's really all the difference is between this groove and Groove 58, but it completely changes the construction and the application.

And that's all well and good, but it's these two great pieces of music that go along with Groove 59 that I want you to focus on. Vashon plays two distinctly different bass lines on this tune; the first time through the form he's right with your bass drum, on the other he's playing a running shuffle rhythm. So you can feel how your syncopations against his downbeat-oriented line create a fantastic rhythmic buoyancy: so much more interesting than simply slamming out quarters on the bass drum. Not that there is anything *wrong* with that…

But hey, look at that: variation A is slamming out quarters on the bass drum! I told you it was cool. Variation B gives you a fresh approach using another syncopation and some ghosts. Note how we're in 4/4 as opposed to 12/8, just so you can see the difference. Either time signature is acceptable and common, so I'm showing you both.

Groove 59 FAST Track 19

Variation A

Variation B

This groove is significantly faster than 58 Fast, so get that right hand ready for a workout. These variations look similar—and they are—but with some important differences, like the slick open hat in variation B.

GROOVE ESSENTIALS 2.0

Variation A

Variation B

CHART

This groove is everywhere, and for good reason—it feels amazing for the band when you get it cooking. Check out how the piano is almost like a drummer on these grooves and listen to his shuffle feel. The guitar, on the other hand, has the freedom to stretch and compress his lines as he wishes. And there you are once again, tying it all together with your perfect shuffle that all the other band members can stand on. Variation B shows you what it looks like with every possible ghost.

FYI: Grooves 58, 59, 60 are often referred to as "blues" grooves, so you could call this a blues shuffle if you like (this is the classic 12-bar blues, after all). People often call the same grooves by different names, so be flexible with your labeling. You know how I feel about labels...

ROCK

Groove 60 FAST Track 21

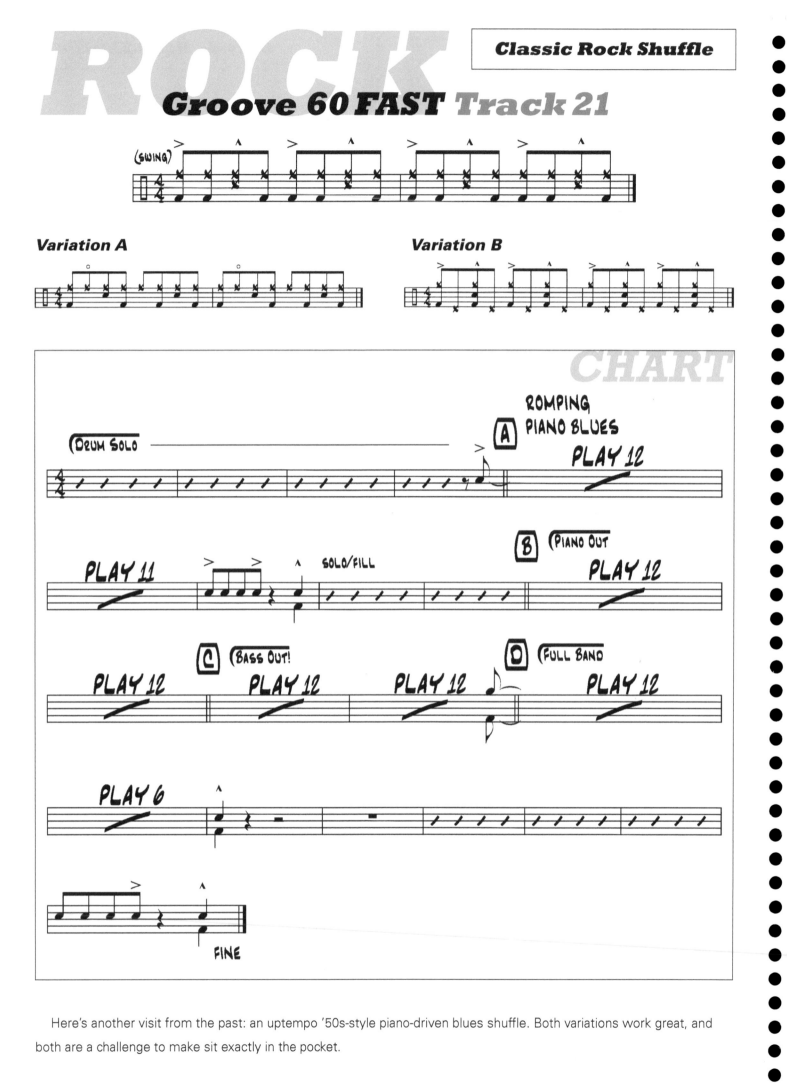

Variation A

Variation B

Here's another visit from the past: an uptempo '50s-style piano-driven blues shuffle. Both variations work great, and both are a challenge to make sit exactly in the pocket.

ROCK

Groove 61 Track 22

Variation A

Variation B

CHART

There's no secret to playing fast grooves: light and tight! Play too loud and it's all over on this burning shuffle. You're the engine, baby.

DRUMSET KEY

	CYMBALS					DRUMS									
RIDE CYMBAL	RIDE BELL	HI-HAT	HI-HAT OPEN	HI-HAT R/SIDE	HI-HAT W/FOOT	BASS DRUM	BASS GHOST NOTE	SNARE	SNARE RIMSHOT	SNARE CROSS STICK	SNARE GHOST NOTE	TOM 1	TOM 2	FLOOR TOM	COWBELL

36

Chapter 2

FUNK Grooves

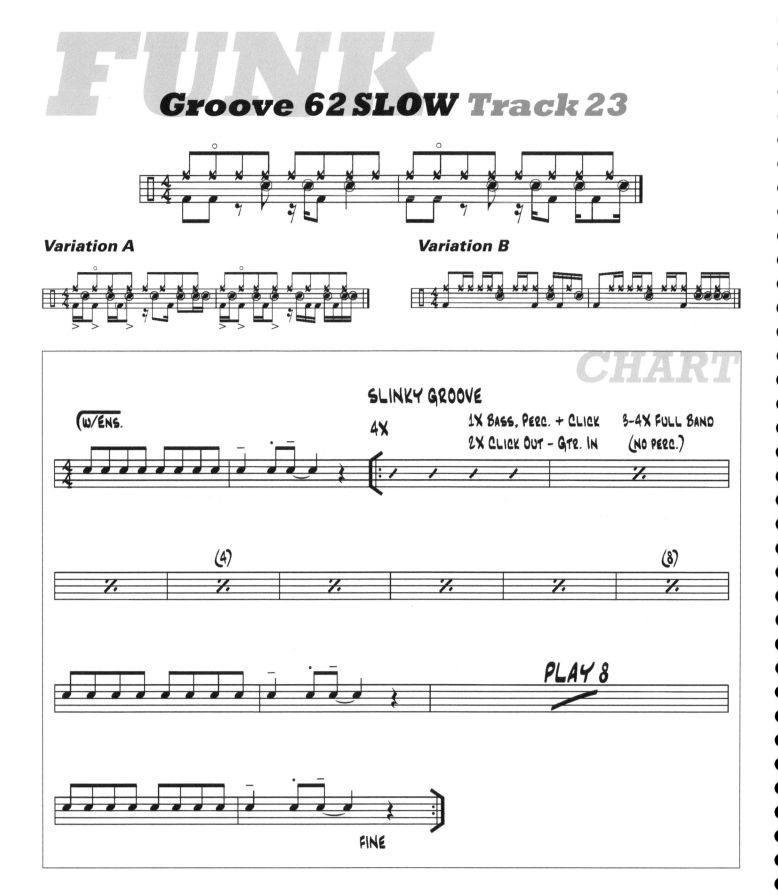

Variation A

Variation B

CHART

SLINKY GROOVE

4X

1X BASS, PERC. + CLICK
2X CLICK OUT - GTR. IN

3-4X FULL BAND
(NO PERC.)

(W/ENS.

(4)

(8)

PLAY 8

FINE

The term "displaced" gets thrown around quite a bit. Displacement is just fancy syncopation, so don't get all intimidated by a word. This is an example of a funk groove with some strong displacement (syncopation), but there is nothing here you can't play if you concentrate and practice with a click first to reinforce the downbeat.

And, being the nice guy I am, I have added a click the first time through the form. But that's it. It's out the rest of way. Notice how the band avoids beat 1 throughout this entire song, creating syncopated lines that match your groove. This is what makes it funky! Variation A is very busy and B is not. Try them both.

FUNK

Groove 62 FAST Track 24

Variation A

Variation B

This groove is a tribute to one of the world's finest drummers, Mr. Steve Jordan, who has played on several of my favorite recordings of all time. This funk groove is inspired by his amazing body of work. I can't recommend strongly enough to listen to anything he plays on.

Even though the tempo is faster here, this one is easier to grab and get a hold of compared with Groove 62 Slow. A great example of why faster tempos are not necessarily more challenging than slow tempos. Quite often, the reverse is true. The secret to why this is easier to hear is simple: the bass is now playing on the downbeat of 1 all the time. That brings your ear into the center of the music and lets you easily identify where "1" is. It's amazing how the parts played by the other instruments affect where the listener will hear the overall downbeat. These displacements—and understanding how to manipulate them—are an incredibly powerful groove construction (and song composition) technique.

Variation A is fun to play because it has that cool little 32nd note on the end of the first bar. Variation B is, well, it's all messed up. It completely displaces everything, and while it's fun to play, it's just like a sharp knife: You'll hurt yourself if you aren't careful.

Groove 63 SLOW Track 25

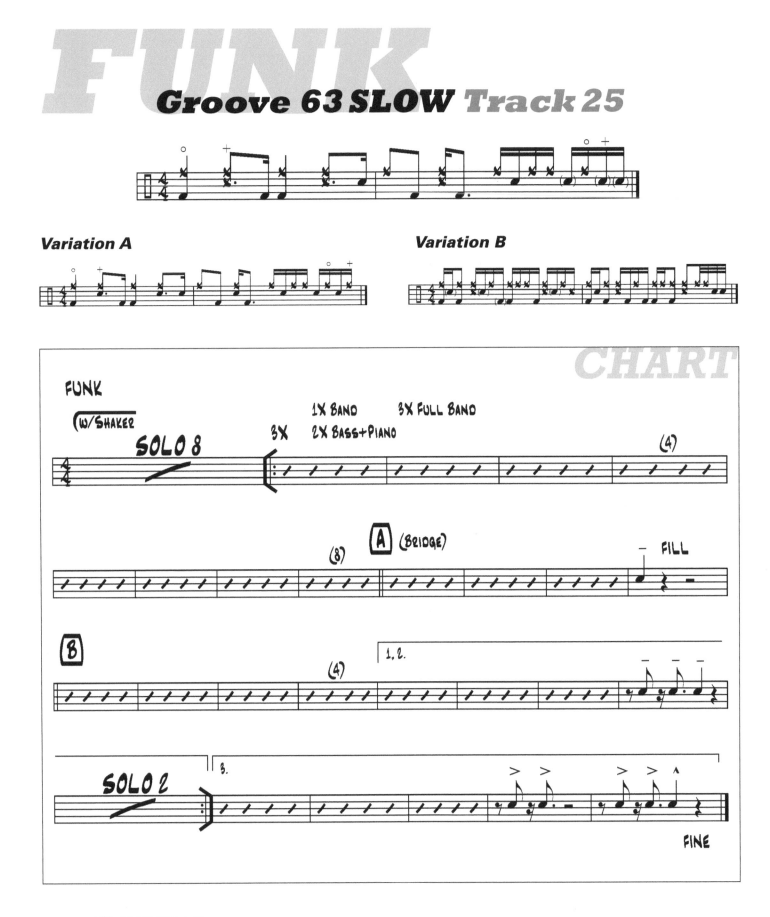

Variation A

Variation B

What can I say about this groove? It speaks for itself. It's dry, it's easy to play, and that little paradiddle thing at the end? Well, people love that stuff… if it's played well. They hate it if it isn't. Paradiddles sound like throwing cans off a roof if you don't execute them properly.

Remember just because you see the word "solo" at the top doesn't mean you don't groove. Think about what your solo is doing here (introducing the song!), so just groove deeply and set up the band. Variations A (which I play on the DVD) and B are both interesting interpretations that you will enjoy.

FUNK

Groove 63 FAST Track 26

Variation A

Variation B

TIGHT FUNK

CHART

Notice how the musicians left a space for the paradiddles at the end of the second bar. See? I told you people love paradiddles. The guitar and keys are also playing a counter-rhythm creating a kind of hypnotic vortex in the middle of the song.

The rhythm on the 2nd and 3rd ending is often referred to as a hemiola (though this is technically incorrect; by strict definition a hemiola must maintain a 2:3 ratio), because it syncopates, repeats, and flows over the barline. Regardless of what it's called, it's a blast to play over. You can really get into serious trouble with this section. In a good way, right? Don't hurt anybody, including yourself.

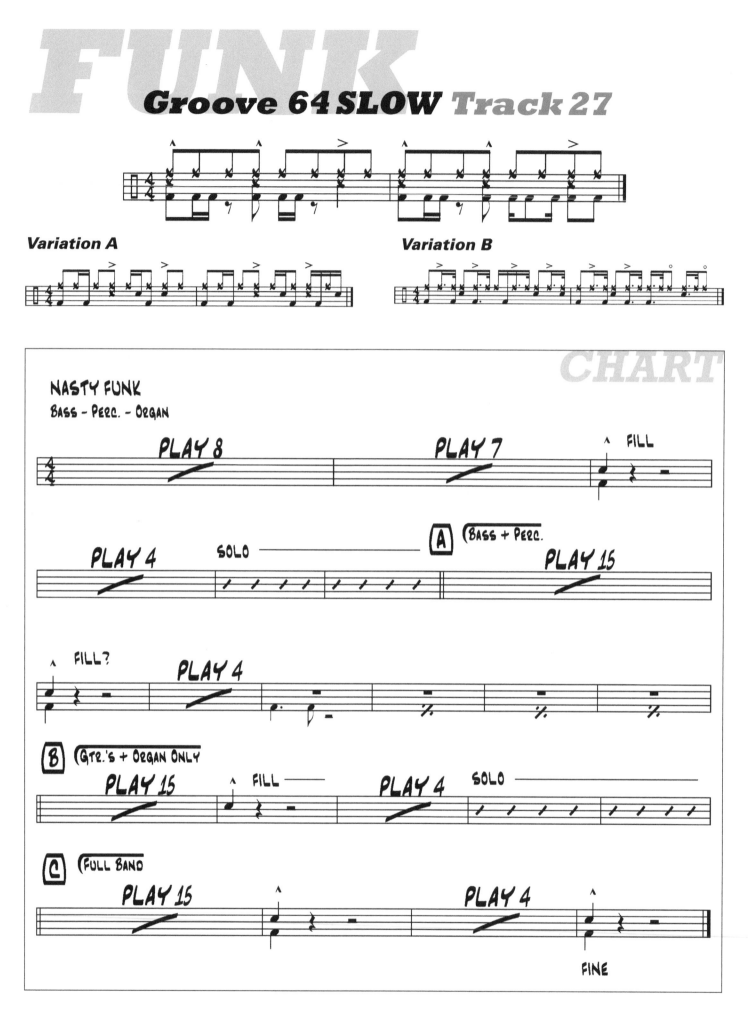

Come on, if you can't get into this groove and track, I don't know what to say. Just the organ part alone is so funky— hear all his ghost notes? And there are three different bass lines to play with, too. The band loves Prince and this was inspired by his amazing work.

FUNK

Variation A

Variation B

CHART

This track is all James Brown! Horns, guitars, bass lines, organs: Man, does it get any better? You are going love this one. Advanced players are going to go nuts with all the solo and interplay possibilities.

Groove 65 Track 29

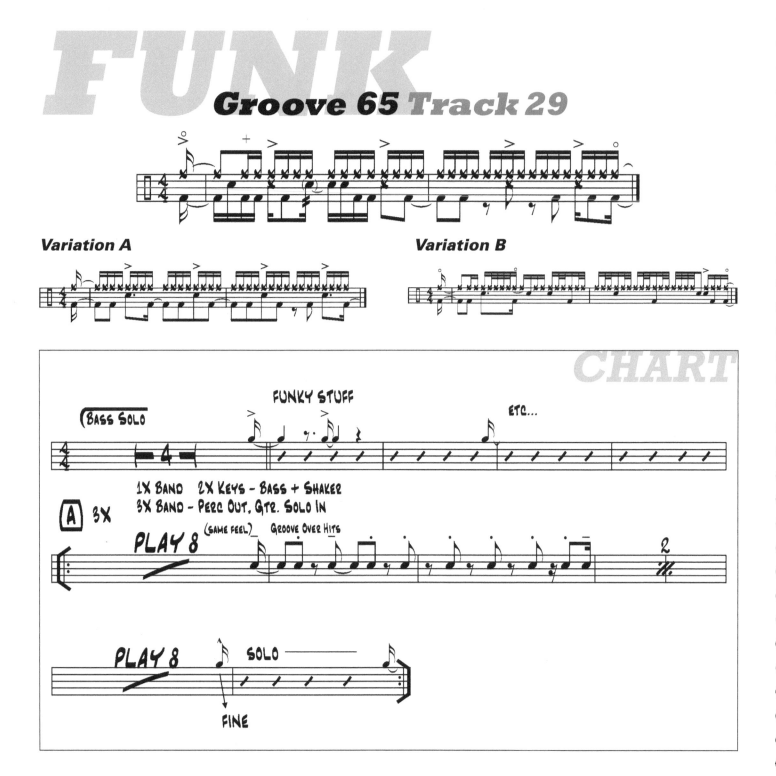

Variation A

Variation B

CHART

Here, we're combining a few different things, but the key groove construction feature is how the groove starts on the last sixteenth note of the phrase. The second bar is also heavily syncopated. Notice how those syncopations actually start on the "and of 4" of the first bar.

When giving dictation exercises to my students, I noticed that the rhythms and grooves that started off the beat were giving them fits, and I understand why. Most of the grooves on our planet, and in *Groove Essentials,* start on beat 1—a very vertical and orderly way to start anything. But as you start to explore more sophisticated music, and certainly music from other cultures, you see grooves that actually avoid starting on 1 (which we already know from exploring the Latin grooves in the original *GE,* right?). Notice how the musicians all reacted accordingly when we came up with this tune. You can hear their phrasing and awareness, and how their parts all obviously lean on the anticipated accent and the internal displacements. Variation B has a scary looking double-time hi-hat part, but it's not as bad as it looks. Well, maybe it is…

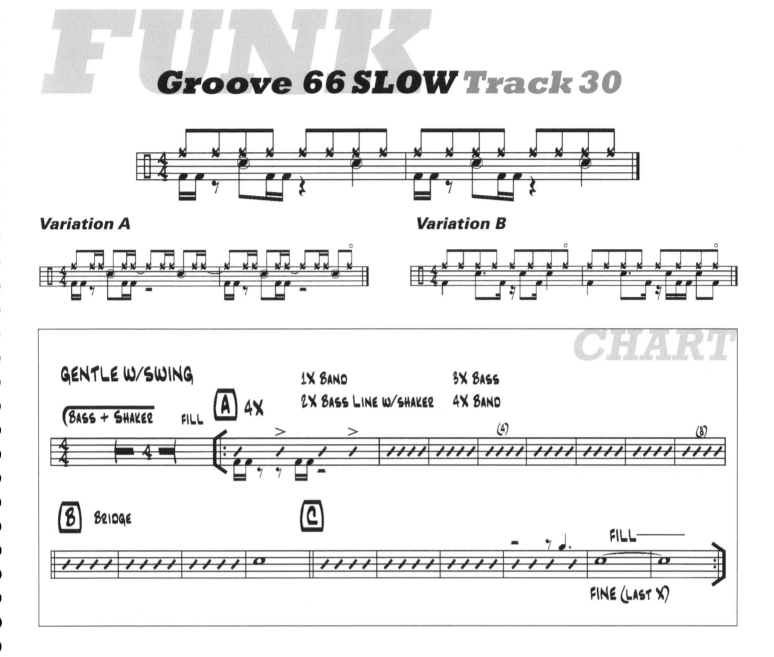

Variation A

Variation B

This funk groove could also easily be in the R&B section. Heck, it could be in the rock section too! The point is, this bass drum rhythm is everywhere. Do you remember a rhythm we discussed in the original *GE* during the Baião Samba called a Charleston? It's a very old rhythm and we're seeing it here again, but now we're doubling each note.

On this track, we're swinging all the sixteenth notes. It's a very, very R&B feel but it's also got some funk to it if you play it right. All these things are just words on a page until you listen to the music and dive in. Please, just don't take this track for granted. Your bass drum control is going to be under some serious scrutiny on this song. There is nowhere to run. You and the bass have to lock up like one person. Record yourself and see if you are.

Variation A avoids quite a few downbeats, which makes the groove lighter. Variation B takes a completely different approach by avoiding the bass line figure altogether and just laying down a complementary groove. Hmmm, very interesting…

Groove 66 FAST Track 31

Variation A

Variation B

CHART

FUNKY SOMETHING
1X BAND
2X BASS + GTR.

PLAY 7

A SMOOTHER PLAY 8

B AS BEFORE
PLAY 7

C FILL/SOLO OVER HITS

D GROOVE
PLAY 8   PLAY 8   PLAY 7

FINE

Ready to test that bass drum foot? Good, here we go. Now, if you want, you could play variation A, which is a fine option if you're foot is not up to snuff for this tempo. Variation B takes the concept of groups of two, and then syncopates them across the bar. It creates a very interesting effect. I would use it as a spice.

Also, note that we are playing perfectly straight on this track and not swinging at all. It takes this groove right back to a more traditional funk place where I think you'll have a great time exploring its many hidden traits.

FUNK
Groove 67 Track 32

This groove is so easy to play I'm almost ashamed I included it here. But, actually, that's *why* I included it here. Who said grooves have to be hard to play to be cool? Our thing is groove construction, and the unique element here is the sticking and how it's just letting your hands flow non-stop. Rather than using intricate patterns, we're using ghosts and rimshots to bring out an internal life all its own. This groove is inspired by one of the funkiest drummers on the planet, Mr. Zigaboo Modeliste. You're going to love how this lays on the drumset.

DRUMSET KEY

CYMBALS						DRUMS									
RIDE CYMBAL	RIDE BELL	HI-HAT	HI-HAT OPEN	HI-HAT R/SIDE	HI-HAT W/FOOT	BASS DRUM	BASS GHOST NOTE	SNARE	SNARE RIMSHOT	SNARE CROSS STICK	SNARE GHOST NOTE	TOM 1	TOM 2	FLOOR TOM	COWBELL

Chapter 3

R&B AND HIP-HOP Grooves

R&B/HIP-HOP
Groove 68 Track 33

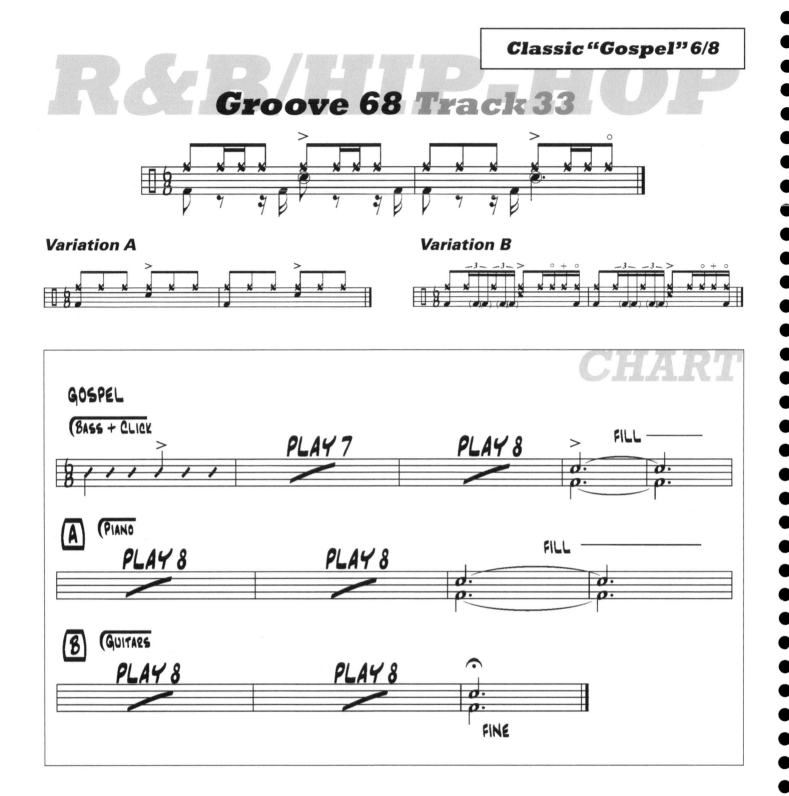

Variation A

Variation B

CHART

GOSPEL

(BASS + CLICK)

> FILL ─────

PLAY 7   PLAY 8

A (PIANO)

PLAY 8   PLAY 8   FILL ─────

B (GUITARS)

PLAY 8   PLAY 8

FINE

This groove should not be thought of like Groove 56, which (you can hear just by listening to its application) is a different groove concept. This is yet again another example of how grooves can look nearly identical on paper and it is *the player's delivery and interpretation* that make the groove appropriate for the style. In short, it's all about the music.

Now, it doesn't say to swing the internal notes, but most of the time you would—and you will here for this track. I've observed that this is one of the defining markers composers will use for popular music written in 3/4 or 6/8. 6/8 often lends itself to a swing feel. But Groove 57 contradicts that—and rightly so—because there are no hard rules for any of this stuff when it comes to time signatures. It's the composer's discretion, and we, as players, need to be ready for anything. Just like sambas can be written in 4/4, 2/4, or 2/2. It's not up to us. Notice that the piano is in the lead: Hear how tight his swing feel is? But he's not playing at the top, so it's up to you to set up the feel for the band. No pressure...

R&B/HIP-HOP
Groove 69 SLOW Track 34

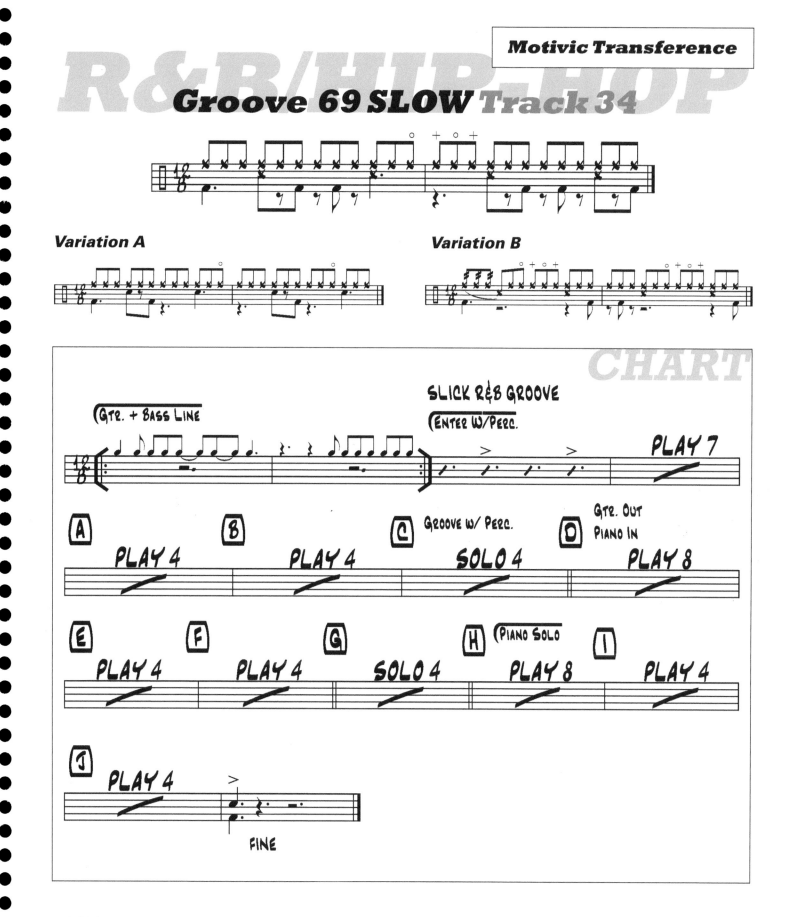

I think you guys are ready for some higher-level construction ideas. *Motivic transference* is a compositional term where you take an idea, or motif, and transfer it somewhere else in the orchestra. Our "orchestra" is the drumset, so we'll take a bass drum motif, transfer it to the hi-hat, and then transfer it back to bass drum, all in the space of two bars.

This track will help you get this groove settled. It's very, very laid back—which is great because this tempo will want to rush ahead. When you listen back (you are recording, right?), don't just listen for whether you are playing the beat correctly (drummer!), but whether you are laying it down exactly in the groove with the track (musician!).

R&B/HIP-HOP
Groove 69 FAST Track 35

Variation A

Variation B

I love the rhythmic base of this song—it's so much fun to play over this guitar and bass line. Watch out for that 3x repeat at letter A on the last time through. What are you going to do with that section? The possibilities are endless! On the DVD, you'll see how I don't change the groove at all at letter A, but you could mix it up and get into all sorts of interesting things if the spirit moves you. Variation B is a good version to play if the motivic transference concept is making you want to jump off a bridge.

R&B/HIP-HOP
Groove 70 Track 36

Variation A

Variation B

The classic "Texas Shuffle!" I must say that Chicago, New Orleans, and Kansas City get in a bit of a snit when they see that the Lone Star State has been given total ownership of this shuffle, but it's not for me to get in the middle of a nearly century-old groove spat. I'm staying out of it. Look, a shuffle is as a shuffle does. You can call it the Swedish Shuffle for all I care; it's not about the name! The song decides the groove, not the other way around. On this one, the guitar solos freely, but the piano (as it often does on shuffles) has plenty to say about the feel—which is a great thing when the incredible Ted Baker is playing the keys. Listen to his shuffle feel!

Extreme Swing

Groove 71 Track 37

Variation A

Variation B

CHART

Listen to the pocket created by the band: It's undeniable; everyone is completely committed to the same swing factor. As a bonus, you get some fun little solo breaks in here, too. Taste! Please, don't just go off. Show some class on those solos.

R&B/HIP-HOP
Groove 72 Track 38

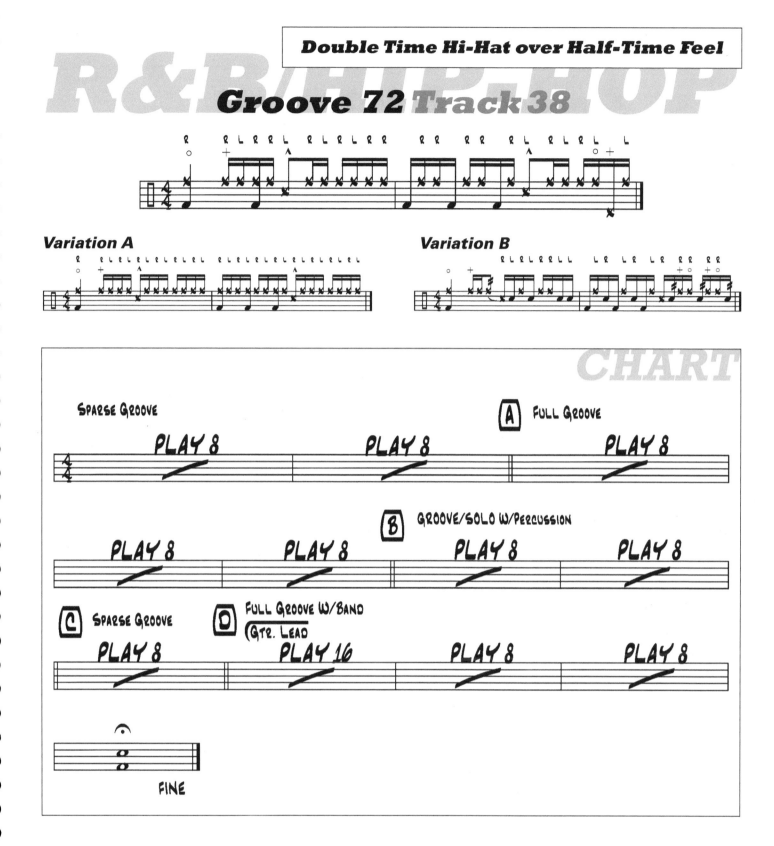

Variation A

Variation B

One of my favorite things about hip-hop drumming—and especially some of the great drummers coming from the church environment—is the use of interesting double-time hi-hat patterns over the top of a half-time feel. It creates this swirling kind of tornado that's a lot of fun to play.

This track will get you playing this type of feel with a very interesting piece of music. We intentionally designed this track to not sound R&B, illustrating how all the families borrow and merge to create new sonic possibilities limited only by your imagination. There is metallic percussion bed that flows through the tune and contrasts nicely with your hi-hat part.

If this hi-hat part is making you queasy, then try variation A. See, there is always a way to get through a piece of music. You just have to be creative. Is it as cool as the original hi-hat stuff? No, but it works. And sometimes you just need something that works. Variation B? Well, it's very cool, and very difficult. You may want to make sure the door is closed.

Groove 73 SLOW Track 39

Variation A

Variation B

There are two masters that are now (and all always will be) associated with this groove: Bernard Purdie and the late, great Jeff Porcaro. They played on legendary tracks that defined the very essence of the ghosted half-time shuffle. But I hope you understand that these great drummers created these grooves for one reason—to musically serve the song they were playing at the moment. They played different shuffles for different songs, which is a point I don't hear discussed often. Listen closely to their great work and you'll hear obvious and subtle differences on various tracks. As you listen, don't just gasp "wow, that's great!" If you desire to be a groove architect, you need to analyze why it's great. Get inside their drumming. Ask questions. What is it about their delivery? The swing? The ghost notes? The balance? Why does it feel so amazing? What is the bass playing? Ultimately, listen to the song, and think of *why* Mr. Purdie or Porcaro played what he did—and then play along yourself.

Variation A is the version to play if the ghosts are giving you trouble. Take your time and practice as slow as you need. Variation B uses only eighths on the hi-hat but with some fancy footwork.

R&B/HIP-HOP
Groove 73 FAST Track 40

Variation A

Variation B

Not only do we get to play a fast half-time shuffle here, but we also see a cool hemiola-like figure that pops up in 3/4. Notice how the band is really sitting up in the pocket on this one. Reflect their energy in your groove. Drive the band!

Variation A has only straight eighths, in case your right hand can't keep up with that nasty shuffle rhythm. Variation B has a slick little open/closed hi-hat thing that works great for these kinds of tempos (if you feel comfortable with it).

From a groove construction standpoint, we've got a few things to talk about with this groove and song. Although this type of groove—a repetitive, syncopated pattern with no backbeat—has been around for a long time, it really got thrust forward when an R&B artist named Sade had a huge hit ("The Sweetest Taboo") using this type of feel. While our groove is quite different, it borrows from the same construction technique.

The song is built on a syncopated dotted-eighth-note bass line. You can hear it being played throughout the entire song, especially when the band plays it in unison, as an ensemble highlight. If you get past all the syncopations of the drum pattern and focus solely on the bass drum part, you'll see the exact line that the bass plays. Also, the second bar of this two-bar pattern is anticipated a sixteenth note early, borrowing from the concept we explored on groove 65.

Look at variation A. Do you see what it is? It's the exact same groove, only with the bass drum and snare parts reversed. Variation B has the hi-hat moving in groups of two with the other parts, making a huge contrast from the main groove.

DRUMSET KEY

CYMBALS — DRUMS

RIDE CYMBAL · RIDE BELL · HI-HAT · HI-HAT OPEN · HI-HAT W/SIDE · HI-HAT W/FOOT · BASS DRUM · BASS GHOST NOTE · SNARE · SNARE RIMSHOT · SNARE CROSS STICK · SNARE GHOST NOTE · TOM 1 · TOM 2 · FLOOR TOM · COWBELL

Chapter 4

JAZZ Grooves

Introduction

In the original *Groove Essentials* jazz chapter, we talked about nine different "grooves" that got us up and running, playing some basic swinging jazz. Today, let's really go in a different direction and take it up a notch or three. I am, of course, assuming you have those basics from the original covered, so please take your time and get those grooves happening first. With *GE 2.0*, we will:

- *Play with, and exorcise, the various myths concerning those scary things with wires that cause so much confusion, intrigue, and fear. Namely—cue scary music—brushes. And, we'll play them at three wildly different tempos, showing three basic patterns that work—and work every time.*

- *We'll take a look at a very common and wonderful thing that happens when you play jazz, where you can take two styles (or more) and throw them into a pot to see what comes out. On today's menu is a jazz mambo, but you can take the idea and apply it to anything you want. Make up something new...*

- *And finally, we'll take a look at surviving an extremely fast swing. In the original GE, as I said numerous times, the term "fast" is intentionally ambiguous since what is fast to you or me may not be fast to someone else and vice-versa. However, this time—I don't care who you are—the piece we're tackling on Groove 79 is fast for everybody and anybody. I told the story on the DVD about the poor student who fell apart at a jam session. Don't worry though, we all have a story like that.*

Until recently, I never understood why brush playing was such a source of frustration for drummers my age and younger. But it all started to make sense when I observed educators call brushes a "lost art," like we've been naughty and misplaced our parents good china. Call me old-fashioned, but I don't think that's a healthy way to start anything. The art isn't lost folks; musical tastes and the art of jazz itself has changed. Even the legends disagree—I witnessed the great Tony Williams declare brushes "a waste of time" in a clinic. While I don't subscribe to that thinking, everyone's entitled to their opinion and it does give a very interesting perspective. Times change, music evolves and drummers play brushes less now for one simple reason: There is less need to. You aren't disrespecting the history of jazz if you can't play great brushes yet; this is simply the reality of our musical era. I'm sure keyboardists thought the world was ending when the harpsichord was replaced with this new-fangled instrument called the—*gasp*!—piano.

Personally, I love playing brushes more than I can say—I think brush playing gives you a fresh perspective on "time"— and I truly believe *anyone* can play them reasonably well. I've come up with a simple, no-frills system to get you up and running without mystery or complexity. After you get these simple patterns happening, you can take your brush playing as far as you want.

After you get these basics down, dig deeper with any book or DVD by two great brush masters: Ed Thigpen and Clayton Cameron, as well as "The Art of Playing Brushes" from Hudson Music.

JAZZ

Groove 75 Track 42

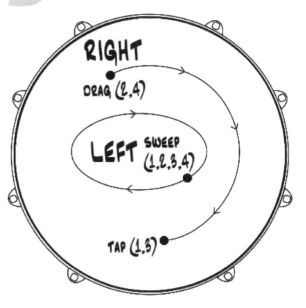

Watch the demo on the DVD if this diagram is confusing. This pattern is a great place to start playing brushes. Start with getting that left hand to "whisper"—seamlessly, gently, gracefully. Your hand should look pretty as it makes the oval shape. If you look or feel tense, shake your arms by your side, breathe deeply and start again. Try the right hand with the "tap-drag" technique. Feel the time! And then try them together. Sound terrible? Of course it does. It always does the first time. This is new stuff! Try again; slowly, gracefully. No rush. Think about hitting your marks on the beats and soon you'll be smooth as silk.

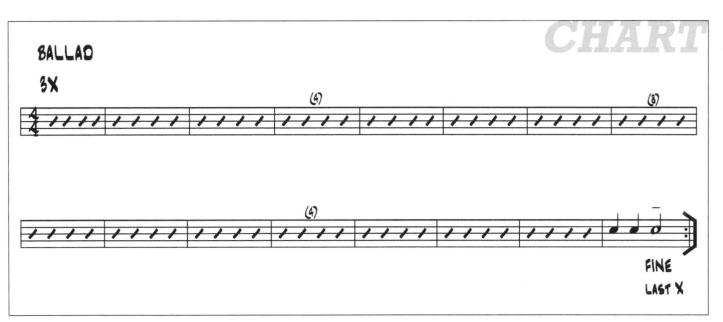

This is a gorgeous, slow jazz ballad. I could just listen to master pianist Allen Farnham play the piano on this track over and over and never get tired of it. Hear his touch? His phrasing? He moves freely between triplet - and duple-based rhythms in his comping and soloing with complete ease. The reason he can do these wondrous things is because you and the bass player are taking care of business. On a tune like this, that means minding the store and not getting pulled off your basic duties of playing the time.

There can be all sorts of great opportunities to play graffiti-like brush patterns, but this, my friends, is most definitely not one of them. This is the time for the piano to shine while we play beautiful, simple brushes in support. Don't forget, you are laying down time for him so he can do his thing. Soft and gentle time, but time nonetheless. Think of it as purpose-driven brushes.

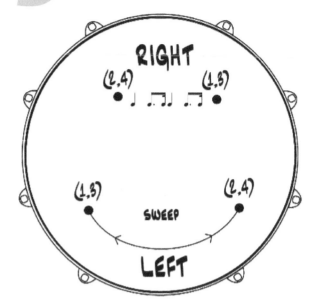

This brush pattern fits perfectly with this medium tempo swing. The left hand sweeps back and forth on the quarter notes, like a windshield wiper. By itself, it's nothing special, but combine it with the right hand playing the jazz ride pattern and it swings like crazy. Feel that "walking" acoustic bass? Your brushes have to lock in with that bass to swing hard. This tempo allows for more brush-pattern experimentation. Listen to brush masters do their thing and emulate the sound of their playing. Err on the side of simplicity when you try new brush strokes. It helps, trust me.

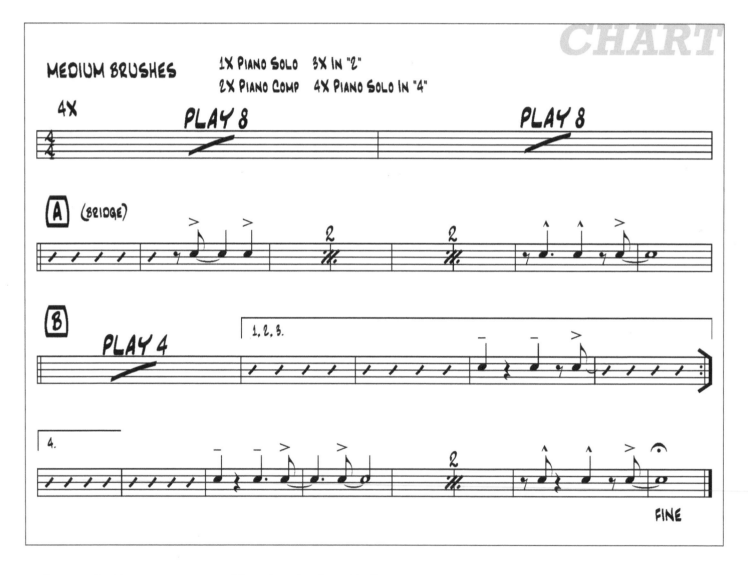

Once again, I have to recommend listening closely to Mr. Farnham on the piano. Hear the feel of his right-hand lines? Let that inspire you to try brush-stroke comping patterns that keep the time moving forward.

JAZZ

Groove 77 Track 44

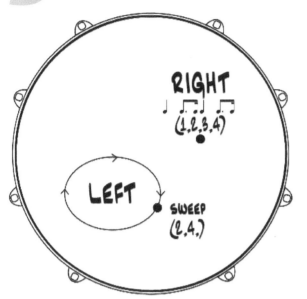

Ready to get those brushes moving? Keep your strokes crisp and pretty. A good brush player looks graceful and effortless, like a dancer. Master drummer Papa Jo Jones looked like Baryshnikov! The tempo of this tune is 285 bpm, which is a nice little clip to be sure. If you can't make it at this tempo, simply stop and get out your friend the metronome. Work it up little by little, day by day, until you start to feel that 285 is no big deal and then slap the track on again. Take your time; there's no rush.

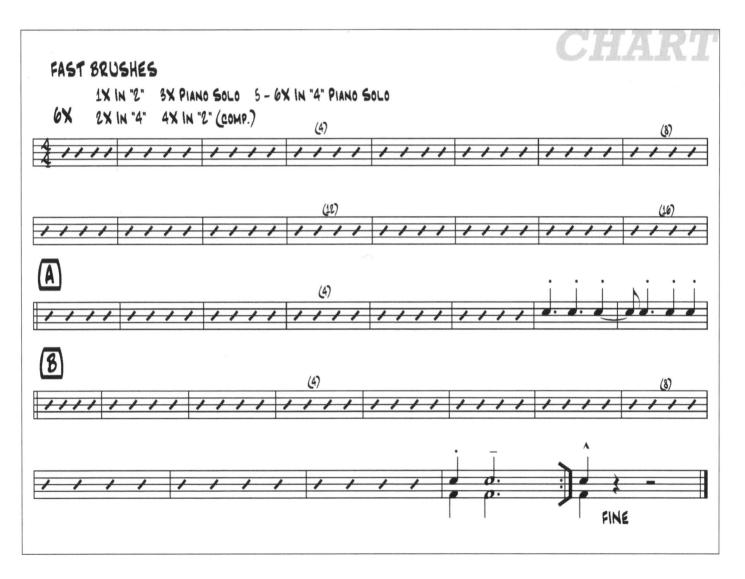

Let's see, we've got you playing in "2," in "4," with a comping piano part, and with a soloing piano part. And if that's not enough, you have to do it while playing brushes at 285 bpm. This one will keep you busy for a bit. Try this song with sticks, too!

You: Swing or straight? Me: I don't know. You: Jazz or Latin? Me: I don't know. Sounds like my private lessons! Look, this is in the crack, in that weird un-writable place between straight and swung, which is why it sounds so cool. Listen to the piano lines and the bass part: the swing feel shifts and morphs. It breathes! Some lines are straight and others are swinging. So, what do you do? You play! You lay down a groove that feels great and allows the breathing going on all around you. Don't strangle the groove or step on the collective feel. Just relax, and let it flow out. Sometimes, no answer is the best answer. Just play…

JAZZ
Groove 79 Track 46

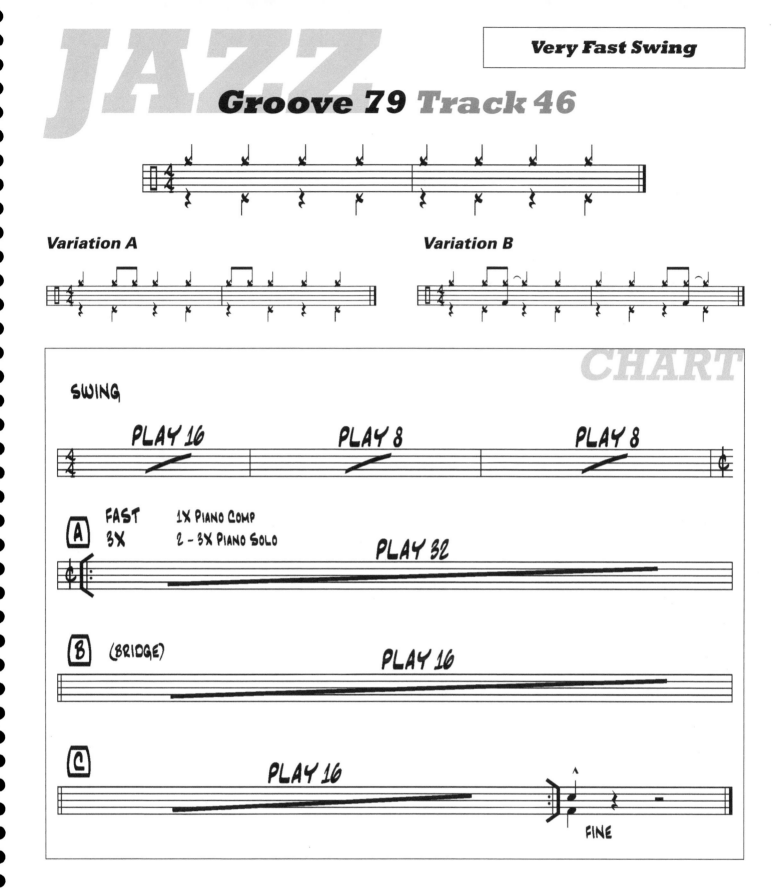

Variation A

Variation B

CHART

SWING

PLAY 16   PLAY 8   PLAY 8

A   FAST   1X PIANO COMP
    3X   2 - 3X PIANO SOLO   PLAY 32

B   (BRIDGE)   PLAY 16

C   PLAY 16   FINE

In the original *Groove Essentials* we topped out at 230 bpm for our "fast" jazz tunes. Here, we're at—are you sitting down?—350 bpm. Yes, that's right: 350 bpm. And if you try to play it like Groove 22 from the original *GE*, you'll need CPR. Groove subtraction again rules the day. Faster tempos need judicious editing to make them swing. So here we're just laying out the basics: the quarter notes on the ride. Listen to great players play really fast tempos and they "dance" on the ride. Variations A and B are both examples of basic ride "dancing." There are about a thousand others limited only by your imagination. You have to experiment with this scary tempo to get it into your hands and mind. Also notice how the chart starts in a medium 4/4 and then jumps to double time after the first chorus. The fun never ends…

DRUMSET KEY

CYMBALS — DRUMS

RIDE CYMBAL · RIDE BELL · HI-HAT · HI-HAT OPEN · HI-HAT R/SIDE · HI-HAT W/FOOT · BASS DRUM · BASS GHOST NOTE · SNARE · SNARE RIMSHOT · SNARE CROSS STICK · SNARE GHOST NOTE · TOM 1 · TOM 2 · FLOOR TOM · COWBELL

Chapter 5

WORLD/ SPECIALTY Grooves

Introduction

oy, have I got some great stuff ready for you in this section! In the original *Groove Essentials,* we had 20 World/specialty grooves that focused primarily on important rhythms from around the world—Afro-Cuban and Brazilian grooves in particular—so that section focused a bit more on "world" than "specialty." This time, it'll be a bit more of an even split, with a specific focus on unique groove construction techniques that have served me well in real-life situations, like when writing the drumset parts for *The Lion King.*

WE ARE GOING TO DIVE IN AND TACKLE THE FOLLOWING GROOVES AND CONCEPTS:

- *Partido Alto*
- *Guaguanco*
- *All-Purpose Latin*
- *Funk Samba*
- *Half-time Afro-Cuban 6/8*
- *The Bo-Diddley Beat*
- *The Train Beat*
- *Rideless Groove (swing)*
- *Rideless Groove (straight)*
- *Rideless Groove (linear)*
- *Cadence*

Please remember what *Groove Essentials* is and (especially for this section) what it isn't. *Groove Essentials* is not designed to be your last stop in your exploration of global genres; it's designed to be your first. My goal is to show you authentic grooves that will inspire you to take the next step and dig deeper into each genre. In *GE 1.0*, I passed along recommendations for books that I personally use with students for further, more in-depth study than what is possible here. Please use them.

This is also the section where your suggestions resonated the loudest. While it was impossible to incorporate all the ideas you sent, I was thrilled that so many of you wanted to learn about some great grooves that I might have overlooked. This section was far and away the favorite in the original book, and it just may be here too. Let's get started.

Partido Alto

Groove 80 SLOW Track 47

Variation A

Variation B

CHART

The partido alto is another type of samba from Brazil. Its unique rhythmic structure is heavily syncopated but (as with most things Brazilian) flows effortlessly like water in a brook. There is no "trick" with sophisticated grooves like a partido alto. It's simply a matter of familiarizing yourself with the language of the style. The internal rhythms have to be as natural as breathing. If you've played nothing but straight-eighth rock grooves your whole life, that can be a challenge in itself. So what do you do?

The first thing you do is listen to the great Brazilian masters. Musicians like Djavan, Gilberto Gil, and Caetano Veloso are constantly bring traditional rhythms like partido alto into their songs. Even if the groove might not be a traditional partido alto in the drumset sense, you can still hear how the root rhythms of Brazil are present in just about everything they do. As I said in the original *GE*, you can't play *anything* with authenticity until you hear the music played by the musicians who know it best.

At this tempo, I am showing you the groove in 4/4 based on sixteenth notes, which is a common way to write this music. Variation A uses a different hi-hat pattern, and variation B incorporates some grace notes.

Partido Alto

Groove 80 FAST Track 48

Variation A

Variation B

CHART

Got your right hand ready to go on this one? Groove 34 from the original *GE* caused a bit of an uproar because of the chops involved with getting out a traditional samba hi-hat part (emulating a pandeiro) using only one hand. This groove is coming from the same place in terms of groove construction; the hi-hat is the panderio again, and the tempo is actually slightly faster than Groove 34. I know, I know... don't hate me. I think you can do it.

Notice any differences compared with Groove 80 Slow? Look closely before I tell you... We're now in cut-time! Traditionally (whatever that means nowadays) we'd be in 2/4, but if you are given a chart in 2/2, you have to be ready. Variation A has a much easier hi-hat part and variation B has a great sounding, though very challenging, hi-hat rhythm. *Thanks, again, to my Brazilian drumming guru, Portinho.*

You can't have a proper World section without something representing Cuba, right? So, let's play the incredible guaguanco. It's not the most popular Latin groove (compared to a songo or mambo), but it has a unique melodic tom-tom part that has a flavor all its own. And since *GE 2.0* is about groove construction, this is a great opportunity to see what a guaguanco offers to expand our vocabulary.

The main groove is the authentic guaguanco (written with a 3:2 rumba clave), but you'll see me gently breaking the rules by applying all the variations throughout the pieces and the demo. The point being you can bend and break some rules, if you know the rules in the first place. That said, if you are playing in an orthodox setting, observe the traditions! It would be disrespectful to start hammering out any old bell pattern. But, if you are going to play in a looser environment, like we are for these pieces, you can start to subtly break outside the box. Use your ears, be sensitive, and you'll be fine. Every time.

Groove 81 FAST Track 50

Variation A

Variation B

CLAVE

CHART

This is a fantastic tune to get your guaguanco to really burn. But it's a different kind of burn on this one; it's a kind of a quiet burn. The dynamic of this track never really gets above mezzo forte and the band's energy is more restrained. You also have a long, long drum solo over a vamp that just builds and builds. This solo will be a real test of your creativity and ability to solo over a piano montuno.

WORLD/SPECIALTY
Groove 82 SLOW Track 51

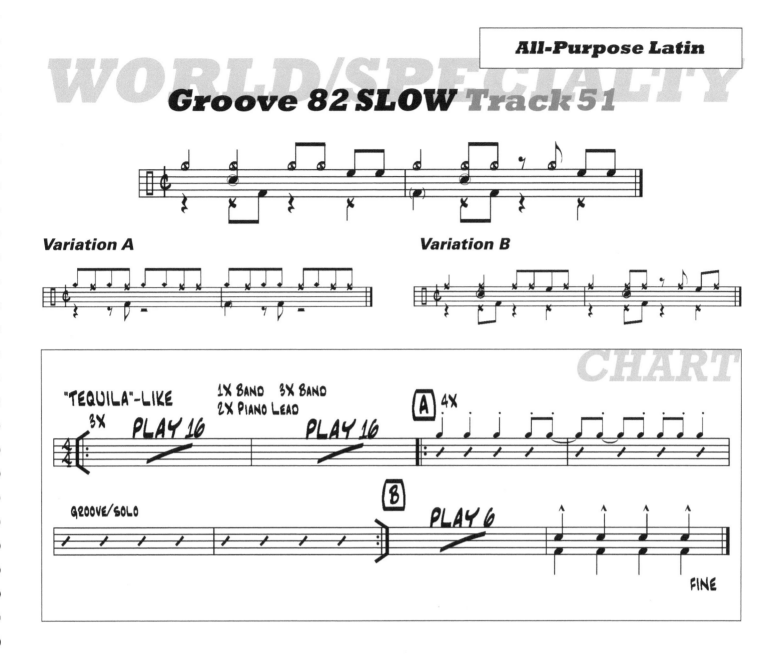

Variation A

Variation B

CHART

"TEQUILA"-LIKE

1X BAND   3X BAND
2X PIANO LEAD

3X   PLAY 16   PLAY 16   A 4X

GROOVE/SOLO   B   PLAY 6

FINE

This just might be the most important groove in the book. Not because it's great (it's not), not because it's impressive (it isn't), but because I would like to slightly ease the fear some of those new to Latin drumming sometimes experience. No disrespect here—authentic knowledge and correct application is crucial—but sometimes you just have to make things work for your situation.

GE is designed to get everyone into the pool. Rockers, meet jazzers; hip-hoppers, meet funksters, and so on. However, many Afro-Cuban grooves and patterns come with such a long and intense history—politics, dance, community, food—that I've seen more than a few students become intimidated. Well, don't be. Approach the music with the respect it so richly deserves, but without fear, and you'll get great results.

Also, sometimes, you just have to tone things down a little from the authentic patterns. Like I said on the DVD, if you are a Latin monster, but the other musicians are struggling, I always think it's a good idea to be a team player and do whatever you have to do to make that situation sound the best it can at that moment. The other musicians will thank you for your mercy.

FYI—this simplified bell pattern is simply a 2:3 cascara with the "and of 4" removed in each bar! So easy...

All-Purpose Latin

Groove 82 FAST Track 52

Variation A

Variation B

CHART

GROOVE ESSENTIALS 2.0

WORLD/SPECIALTY

Groove 83 Track 53

Variation A

Variation B

As I said on the DVD, this groove is a tribute to one of the finest groove players ever, Mr. Carlos Vega. When I was in my early teens and practicing with my favorite records, I noticed he was on many of them. His groove was amazing, and because I never got a chance to meet him and tell him how much I loved his drumming, I'd like to honor him here. Search his name and check out his great playing!

When I toured with the great Dave Grusin, we played a tune that Carlos recorded. The groove defied any kind of name; I didn't know what to call it. When I got the chart, it simply said "funk samba." All I could think was, "Carlos is a genius!" So here's a groove, a smash-up of funk and samba, inspired by his fantastic drumming.

WORLD/SPECIALTY
Groove 84 Track 54

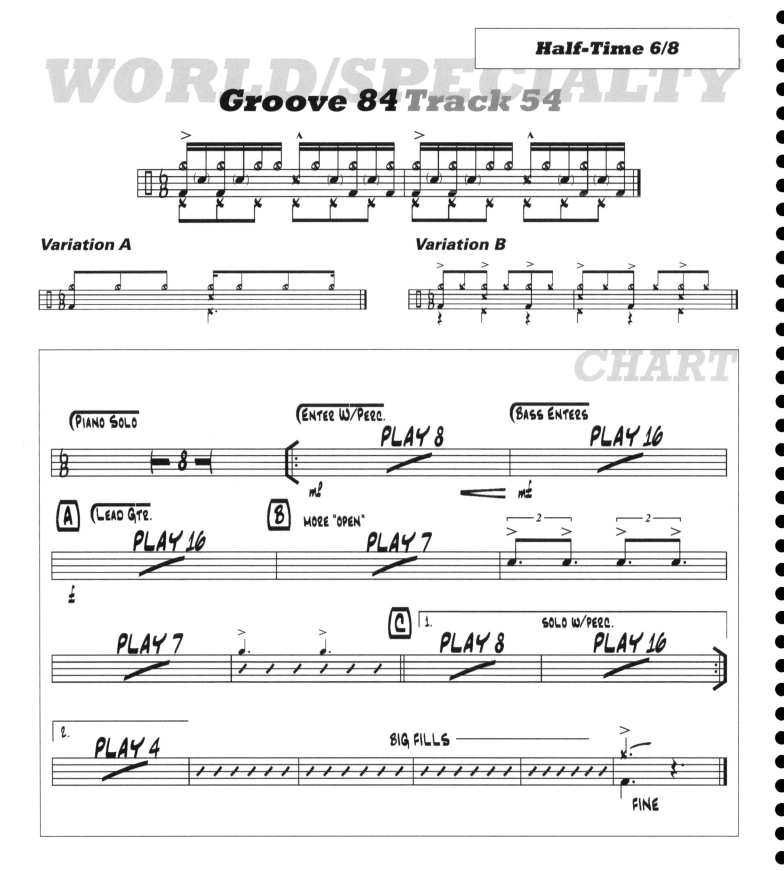

Variation A

Variation B

CHART

We learned an Afro-Cuban 6/8 groove in the original *GE* called a Nanigo. But what if you took the "African" portion in the right hand and combined it with a half-time backbeat in the left? That's the feel that Groove 84 introduces—a very common kind of groove hybrid (especially in modern jazz and rock). As with many African-based rhythms, it's written in 6/8 but can be felt in "four"; I count it off on the DVD that way to show you the contrast.

Really listen to and appreciate all the musical elements going on in this track: busy percussion, a quasi-classical running piano part, very spacious bass, and a screaming guitar solo over the top. This one is going to keep you busy.

Variation A is completely stripped down and features a slightly different bell pattern, while variation B features a slick way to displace the time by simply phrasing in groups of two. Think of it like hot red pepper: a little goes a long way.

If there is a more obvious example of how the delivery of the groove separates good from great musicians, I don't know what it is. Bo Diddley was one of the original blues pioneers who made an integral contribution in the transition from old-school blues to the "new" rock era in the 1950s. He recently passed on, but his contribution to music will be with us forever. Bo did not invent this rhythm (it's a 3:2 son clave), he didn't invent the chords (often a basic blues), but he invented the application, delivery, and (more importantly) the overall groove! Although this groove appears simple, notes written on a page will never be able to convey the commitment you need to bring it to life.

The interesting construction element here is that we are staying on one drum. 99% of drumset playing is built on multiple layers playing independent rhythms to create an overall groove. Not here. This groove creates a completely different sound quality that you need to appreciate so you can use it appropriately when you play in your own bands.

This song features the groove in its glorious simplicity, with a Bo Diddley "box" guitar as the prominent sonic feature. Very lo-fi, very dirty, and very cool. As you'll undoubtedly hear, the musicians had a blast making this track.

WORLD/SPECIALTY

Groove 86 Track 56

Variation A

Variation B

CHART

(GUITAR ALONE)

A BLUES
TRAIN! (GTR. LEAD)
PLAY 24   PLAY 22

B (PIANO LEAD)
PLAY 24   PLAY 22   SOLO

C (PIANO + GTR. SOLO TOGETHER)
PLAY 24   PLAY 22

FINE

Ready to get on the Train? Incidentally—and this is the for R&B police out there— the Bo Diddley and Train beats both technically belong in the R&B section, but I'm putting them in the "specialty" family because they have been given brand names that are indisputable. You may find musicians who call a "Texas shuffle" by another name, but not this baby. This groove is the Train to me, you, and the rest of the world. It's a special groove, so it resides here.

Like the Bo Diddley beat, the way the Train looks on paper can't even begin to show the feel of the groove. It's just like learning jazz: if you are trying to learn jazz drumming patterns from a book without listening to jazz, the notes on the page will come out sounding like exercises. Same thing here. If you hear the music played by master musicians, and get that sound in your ear, you can then play the notes on the page as they were intended. It is important to listen to great Nashville drummers play the Train beat. But be aware that as country music evolves and changes, "classic" grooves like the Train beat are getting harder to find on new recordings. There is live concert footage of some great Nashville drummers playing the Train beat on YouTube; do a search and you'll see what I mean.

When I told our great guitarist, Kevin Kuhn, we were doing a Train beat and I wanted the guitar to lead the way, he was like a little kid on Christmas morning. You'll hear why...

WORLD/SPECIALTY
Groove 87 SLOW Track 57

Variation A

Variation B

CHART

SNEAKY SWING
(W/ENS.)

FILL?

FILL?

FINE

A 2X-BASS OUT

1.
PLAY 8   PLAY 24

2.
PLAY 6   FILL

(W/BASS
PLAY 16   **B** 4X-DRUM SOLO

(CLICK 1-2X)   ETC...

(BAND W/GTR. SOLO
PLAY 32

D.C. AL FINE

While writing the drumset book for Broadway's *The Lion King*, we had a great producer (Mark Mancina), who despised "normal" drumming. "Too ordinary!" he'd scream at me. I quickly learned that any metallic ride (hi-hat or any cymbal) was the offending characteristic, so I was basically forced to come up with grooves that were "rideless." New grooves that had a different flavor unlike anything I had played or written before.

Although the Bo Diddley and Train beats are also "rideless," they are grooves that have already been defined by their respective genres. Here, we are talking about creating new grooves.

Groove 87 is a groove that reverses many of the aspects of normal drumming. We're going to be playing a running shuffle with our left hand while the right hand plays the primary accent pattern (with ghosts). The feet stay simple, playing downbeats and upbeats.

The next four pieces of music were inspired by the grooves you're about to play. Notice how the musicians came up with parts that are different from their normal roles. I'm sure you'll love playing along to these unique tracks.

Groove 87 FAST Track 58

Variation A

Variation B

CHART

Get that left hand ready for this one. Variation A will give you an option if your left hand can't quite keep up. Variation B is an exact transcription of an "implied metric modulation" fill I play on the DVD. I really try to stay away from this stuff on the *GE* videos, but this one slipped out. For advanced players, I say give it a try!

WORLD/SPECIALTY
Groove 88 SLOW Track 59

Variation A

Variation B

CHART

Here is a completely different example of rideless construction. This groove is based on the right hand playing a melodic accented tom pattern, with the left hand filling in all the ghost notes. The left hand also plays the primary rimshot accent on the "ah" of beat one.

If you want to truly understand the power of rideless construction, try playing this track with a "normal" R&B groove, like Groove 14 from the original *GE*. Yuck! It's like sticking a square peg in a round hole. All that metal from the hi-hat just doesn't work on this velvety-smooth song.

Both variations add or subtract something from the main groove, but it really is the main groove that is the star here, and I wouldn't use the variations for anything more than an occasional spice. This is a fantastic example of how rideless construction not only makes your drumming sound different, it can affect the entire vibe of a song.

History note: I certainly didn't invent rideless drumming. Most contemporary drummers are unaware that the early versions of the drumset didn't even have a "ride" cymbal, so by modern standards, all grooves were rideless. In fact, the term "ride cymbal" was not coined until after Word War II, decades after the first drumset "contraption" was invented.

Rideless: Straight

Groove 88 FAST Track 60

CHART

Your pattern—your rideless groove—is the star of this song. It's the constant flow coming from the drums that propels this tune and makes it soar. The musicians, being the sensitive players they are, leave a ton of space on this track.

Here's another important concept I work on with students: You don't have time to settle into a groove; it has be ready to go from the very first note you play. It's easy to stumble around the first four bars and get things to settle into a groove by bar five. No, not acceptable! It has to be great from the first note. If you accept the first bars being poor, they will always be poor. Jettison that amateurish thinking from your mind like rotten food from your mouth. Accept only great drumming from yourself and you'll soon notice your playing rise to another level. It really is that simple.

GROOVE ESSENTIALS 2.0

WORLD/SPECIALTY
Groove 89 Track 61

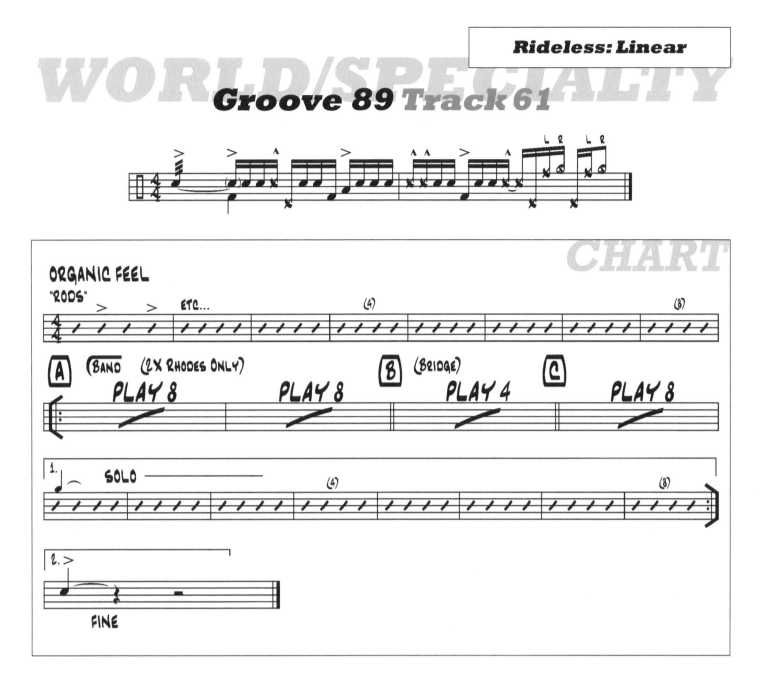

When you play gigs with singer/songwriters, many times you'll have to provide a soft, "organic" kind of groove. I guess it can be described as a groove that is ultra-acoustic: warm and soft around the edges. This groove is the opposite of a sharp, staccato-type groove, like Groove 51. It again has that rideless flow that you can't get from normal ride-based drumming.

This pattern features more of a "linear" approach (check out Gary Chaffee's great books to learn all about this fantastic style of playing) where one limb is playing at a time.

We are playing with multi-rods on this song, and I can't recommend the Vic Firth Rute 505 model enough. They bend, but you still "hear" the drum, and they get a great slappy sound. Sticks would be totally inappropriate for the vibe we're trying to create here.

When you play this groove, try not to be obsessed with being rudimentally perfect. I'm not telling you to play sloppy, but I am suggesting that if you want to fatten the pocket of this groove, you can pick and choose parts of the groove on which to lay back. It creates a more pliable vibe that lets you explore your unique groove personality.

There are no variations here because this groove is a finished concept and a definitive part of the fabric of the song. The musicians molded this, without any coaching on my part, into a very "country" kind of song. Isn't that pedal steel guitar fun to play with? The groove inspired them to make this music, and I was fascinated and ultimately very satisfied to see where it went. This truly stands out as a unique piece of music in the library of *Groove Essentials* songs.

Military Cadence

Groove 90 Track 62

As the proud son of a great drummer, I hope you'll indulge me for just a moment. This "groove" is a nod of love and respect to my father, Sonny Igoe, a master drummer and legendary educator who was—and still is—a great example to me and the thousands of private students who flowed through his studio over a 50-year teaching career. As my own teaching genes kicked in, I sent my serious students (you know the ones—they sleep with their sticks) to see Sonny for a few lessons. I would just tell them to "absorb it all." The stories, the history, the guidance—just watching a pro *function*—is priceless training. He is a living glimpse of an era that, in stark contrast to modern times, needed expert musicians to get any musical work done. Sonny played this cadence on a recording session for the NFL. It was simply the drums and the NFL logo slowly coming up on screen, and he made this cadence groove so hard, it felt incredible! I can't think of a better example of how everything, without exception, must groove.

Now, I've always loved rudimental drumming, and when I was a kid I played in drum corps, and all the stuff we played was much harder and hipper than this simple cadence—and that's the point. I've seen drummers who could eat swiss-cheesed-reversed-pataflafla'd-eggbeaters for breakfast, but couldn't make this simple cadence feel good on a drumset. It's a different set of chops.

Play this as it looks on paper, it will sound like a bunch of vanilla rudiments strung together, and that is not what we want. Sonny picked this up from his time in the U.S. Marine Corps in World War II, passed it on to me, and I'm honored to share it with you here. I hope you enjoy playing it, and perhaps you'll get a gig from it too, like I did. Thanks, Sonny...

For you guys without a metronome (which I'm sure is very few, right?), I'm giving you enough click on this track for two times through the form at 110bpm.

DRUMSET KEY

CYMBALS — DRUMS —

RIDE CYMBAL | RIDE BELL | HI-HAT | HI-HAT OPEN | HI-HAT R/SIDE | HI-HAT W/FOOT | BASS DRUM | BASS GHOST NOTE | SNARE | SNARE RIMSHOT | SNARE CROSS STICK | SNARE GHOST NOTE | TOM 1 | TOM 2 | FLOOR TOM | COWBELL

Chapter 6

ODD METERS

Introduction

**A**h-ha! You just couldn't wait, could you? Come on, admit it, I'll bet you haven't even come close to hitting all the grooves before these, right? Well, I don't blame you; I would have done the same thing too. In fact, an odd-meter chapter was by far the most requested item from users of the original *Groove Essentials*, by a ratio of 5 to 1! I have to admit I was thrilled, since I'm an odd-meter addict myself. I find few things more musically exciting than watching a group of great musicians play gracefully in an odd meter. And let's face it, it's just fun to break out of the normal 4/4 thing once in awhile. You don't eat the same thing every day, right?

As I said in the introduction (you did read the intro, right?), you really need to have your common time (4/4) stuff together if you want to have success here. Here's the thing about 4/4: unless you grew up in a culturally isolated place—and as the world shrinks there are fewer all the time—you've been slammed over the head with 4/4. Even if you spent your life in places that feature odd meters as part of the culture, 4/4 is inarguably the popular sound of the world. You simply can't escape it. And that's fine, it's not like 4/4 is some sort of odd-meter poison, it just means that your ear is tuned a certain way. I believe that it's always best to approach new concepts from a position of strength, and knowing why something will be a challenge puts you in the drivers seat—instead of floundering around helplessly wondering why something is hard. This stuff is NOT hard, it's NOT a mystery, and if you take your time and stay positive, I WILL have you playing in odd meters—guaranteed.

As with all genres, some drummers pick up odd meters faster than others. If you've never played odd meters before, this has the potential to be a very frustrating chapter at first. But I'm going to outline three essential things that will help you. Now, this is a long and confusing list, but I think you can handle it. This really is the solution to anyone's odd-meter problems. Ready?

1. Count!
2. Count!
3. No, seriously. Count!

Get it? Now, I know it's all educationally chic to say "just feeeeelllll the music!" and that's great advice if indeed you can actually feel the music, but what if you can't? What if you don't know where 1 is, and you just can't feel it? You get proactive. Sometimes 1 is like a two-year-old toddler in the park: It won't come to you; you have to go get it. Which brings us to...

The Golden Rule of Odd-Meters

Do you want success in playing odd-meters? Then repeat after me:

Thou Shalt Not Guess!

I've watched drummers stumble over these grooves suffering needless frustration all because of committing the worst possible odd-meter sin: Guessing! Don't *guess* where 1 is, *know* where 1 is. You can't aim for 1 like it's a game of darts! How do you stop aiming? How do you stop guessing? Count out loud. Shouting out loud is fine too. Do whatever it takes to get the feel of the meter into your mind and body. Once you get it, count softer and softer. Soon you won't be counting out loud anymore—you'll be feeling the groove by that point—but there is no rush. Need to count out loud? Do it! If you guess, you're done. It's that simple.

In *GE 2.0* we'll be looking at some funk in 3/4, and then three different levels of 5, 7, and 9. Odd meters can go as high as you like—the longest I've ever played was 21 (which I secretly broke into a 9+5+7 so my brain wouldn't flame out). I've noticed 9 to be a kind of "Eureka!" meter for musicians, since it's usually dealing with four split subgroups. If you can function in 9, you can pretty much take things as far as you like. Just remember it's about music, not math. The ultimate goal is to make this "odd" stuff seem "normal," meaning it just flows effortlessly without any hiccups or stutters. Your audience shouldn't even know anything "odd" is going on.

In the description text for each odd meter, I'll tell you the breakdown of how to count that particular groove. And as a bonus, your disc has extra tracks that feature a vocal counting along with the basic 5, 7, and 9 songs. For those who are just really having a hard time getting this whole odd-meter thing together, these tracks will really help. I absolutely guarantee you will get it if you persevere and take your time. I wrote these grooves very carefully, and they are designed to have you taste different kinds of odd meters and their possible musical applications. Of course, there are so many more. Now that you're playing in odd meters, go out there and get some more music to practice with! Three great and diverse recommendations are: Sting's *Ten Summoners Tales*, Frank Zappa's *Joe's Garage* (it's tough to listen to but the genius is undeniable), and Dave Holland's *Global Citizen*. Also, if you want to make your head explode (in a good way), check out any Mahavishnu Orchestra or Shakti recording (Shakti contains no drumset, but every drummer needs to hear tabla master Zakir Hussain).

On a personal note, a real honor for me were the e-mails requesting odd-meters from those who were slugging their way through the first Groove Essentials. They made a point to tell me that because GE gave them the tools and confidence to play a samba or a songo, they wanted the same "no-nonsense, practical application" concept applied to odd meters. I was thrilled. As an educator/author, you can't get a bigger compliment than people asking for more of your work.

If you are serious about mastering odd-meters, and you really want to explore freeing your mind, learn, as I have, the Indian Konokol system of counting rhythms. Study with the incredible DVD A Gateway to Rhythm by John McLaughlin and Selvaganesh Vinayakram. It will push your concept of time and rhythm to another level! It's the next best thing to having a personal Konokol expert walk you through the concepts.

Funk in 3

Groove 91 Track 63

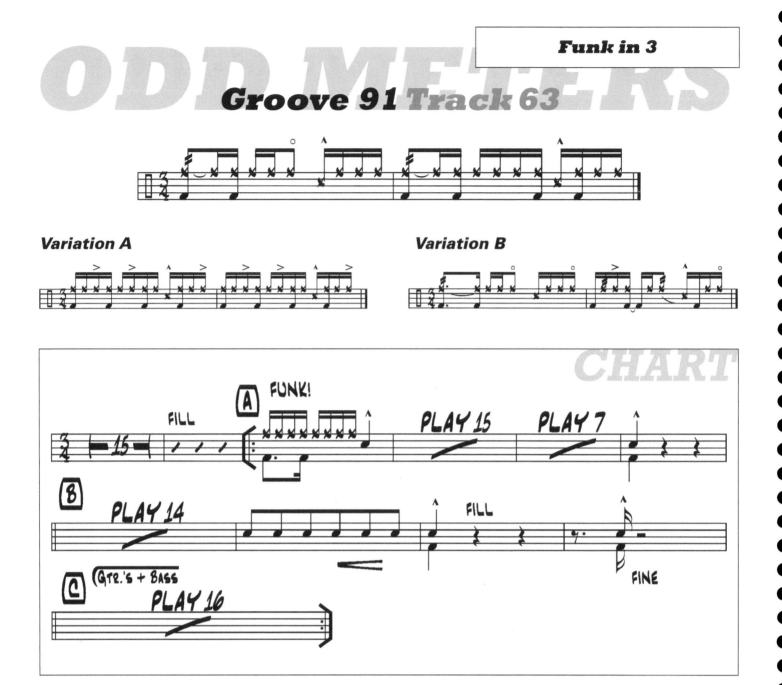

Variation A

Variation B

CHART

To kick us off into our odd-meter frenzy, here is a little something that is familiar, but skewed in a slightly different way. You and I have been playing in 3 for quite awhile now (counting the 6/8 grooves, this the 10th groove in 3 that we are exploring together), but this time we're going to play in a syncopated funk style.

Playing a funk in 3, as opposed to 4, highlights how different things sound and feel when you knock them out of 4/4. The whole thing lays in your hands and on the drumset in a unique way. You'll feel it the moment you start to play the pattern.

This song lends itself to playing all sorts of interesting hi-hat work if you choose to do so. I demonstrate some of this on the DVD; feel free to improvise on your own as well. Variation A is one of those implied 4-over-3 polyrhythms I demonstrate on the DVD that you can try—or not. No pressure. The interesting thing about it is that the polyrhythm starts on beat 3 instead of the usual beat 1. Variation B has some rolling hi-hat work that, obviously, you would only use as a spice, not as a repetitive main groove.

As the piano sets up the song (we have 15 bars rest!), listen to his feel, and then, as you play your fill on bar 16, ask yourself if you set the pocket up perfectly for the band. That's what that fill is all about.

Remember, even though 3 is an odd number, grooving in 3 is such a common requirement that you can't realistically think of it as something odd. But for those beginning to get into the world of odd meters, 3 is a fun and inviting introduction.

GROOVE ESSENTIALS 2.0

ODD METERS

Groove 92 Track 64

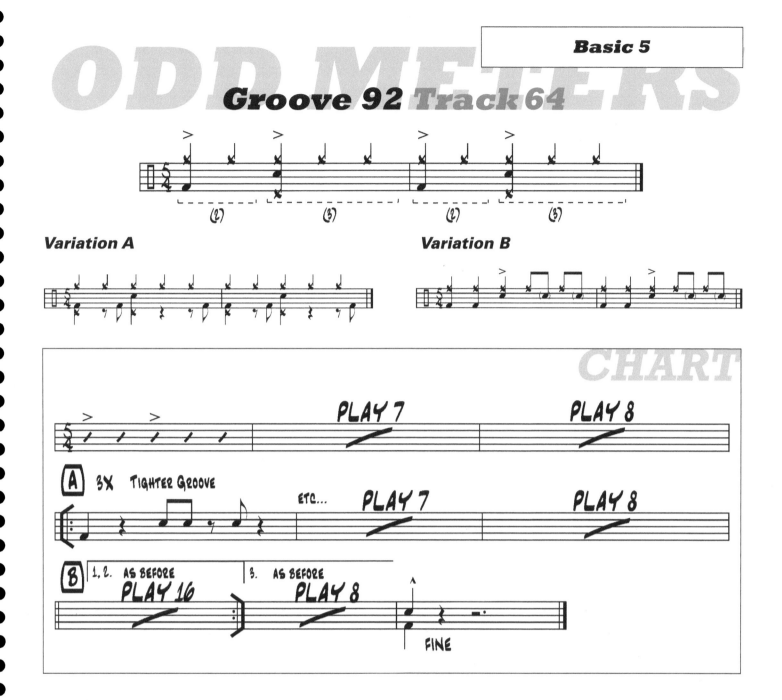

Variation A

Variation B

Okay, most will consider this the first real odd-meter groove in the book, and so do I. This basic 5 could not be simpler, and you'll have no problem getting it going. But if you do, remember:

Count!

Count!

Count!

And we always split odd meters into groups of 2 and 3. The band is leaning hard on the groupings for our basic 5: a group of 2 and a group of 3. Count it with me on the DVD if you are lost. If you listen to the music and hear their parts, the outlining structure of the groove is obvious. Just join in with the main groove, and you'll be playing in 5!

The tunes for the basic odd meters (grooves 92, 95, and 98) are designed for one purpose only: to get you to feel the meter in an obvious and musical fashion. The hip stuff will come later, but you can't do the hip stuff if you can't function with confidence here. Take your time!

Remember— use the extra track with vocal counting on your disc if you are having any problems feeling this groove.

ODD METERS

Groove 93 Track 65

CHART

Things are heating up, and we've arrived at an intermediate 5 (split into a 2-3 pattern). Again, as with all the descriptive terms I use, "intermediate" is intentionally ambiguous. Some will think this groove is impossibly difficult, while others will just eat it up. In terms of groove construction, we have several interesting features here, starting with the hi-hat. Notice the open hi-hat on 1 in the first bar with a long quarter-note length: an unusual and highly effective place for an open hi-hat. Also, it's a two-bar groove with more motion in the second bar to answer the long hi-hat in the first bar.

Variation A (written in 5/8 for notational variety) has a hi-hat figure that flows over the bar line, and variation B is an exact transcription of the implied double-time figure I play at the very end of the song on the DVD.

ODD METERS
Groove 94 Track 66

Variation A

Variation B

Now, let's kick a 5 up through the roof. Notice we are in 5/8—by the way, the bottom number in a time signature is up to the composer, not you. Be ready for anything, and be sure you are counting appropriately.

On the DVD, I demonstrate both the main groove and variation A. Because of this song's fast tempo, variation A is the best choice. Variation B is the main groove written in 10/16. Now, 10 may not be considered an odd number, but that groove sure looks odd to me! That's why "odd" means "not ordinary," not "non-even." Could it be written that way for real? Of course, that's why you must be ready for anything, because anything can happen.

ODD METERS
Groove 95 Track 67

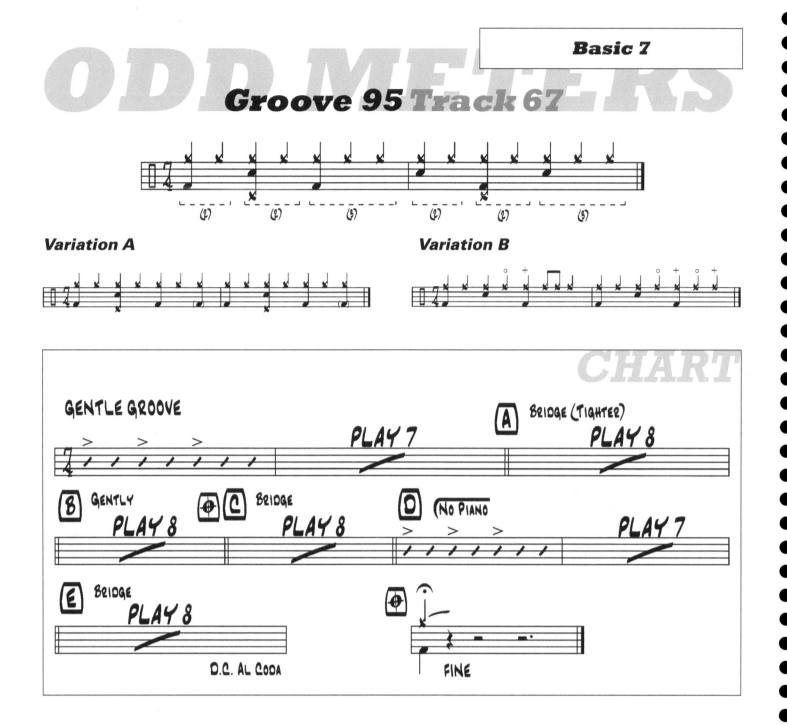

Variation A

Variation B

CHART

GENTLE GROOVE

PLAY 7

A BRIDGE (TIGHTER)
PLAY 8

B GENTLY
PLAY 8

C BRIDGE
PLAY 8

D (NO PIANO)
PLAY 7

E BRIDGE
PLAY 8

D.C. AL CODA

FINE

Here we are at 7, everyone's favorite odd meter. There is just something about 7 that musicians enjoy; perhaps because it's easy to play (I've found drummers grasp 7 very quickly). Whatever the reason, 7 is the meter likely to be called out on jam sessions if you've got some wacky guy who wants to do something different. "Hey, let's play "My Funny Valentine" in a fast Latin 7!" Ya never know…

As with the basic 5, the groupings in the main groove are outlined for you to help visualize the counting. You have two groups of 2 and one group of 3. The counting will be: 1-2-1-2-1-2-3. Count it just like I do on the DVD, and you'll have absolutely no problems whatsoever. If you do have trouble, play with the bonus track on the disc, which features this song and a vocal counting track running throughout.

As always, listen to the musicians! They are laying out that simple basic 7 for you by playing all the 1s of your counting pattern. Variation A adds a little setup note in the bass drum, and variation B is played on the hi-hat rather than the ride.

ODD METERS
Groove 96 Track 68

Who said odd meters have to be straight-eighth-note based? Let's really go nuts and play a half-time shuffle in 7 and see what trouble we can get ourselves into. We're again in a 2-2-3 counting pattern, but the tempo is actually slower, since we're now basing this groove on a smaller subdivision than the previous basic 7.

A quick clarifier on time signatures, in case I haven't made it clear: You should be able to read and play in any time signature. In fact a good drill would be to take, for example, this 7/8 groove and write it out in 7/4 and 7/16, just to see what it looks like. I've had so many charts where I've wondered, "why didn't he write it in x/x? It would make so much more sense." But apparently not to the composer/arranger, and that's all that matters. I'm choosing solid ways to write these songs for you, but just keep in mind, it could be in another time signature and still be completely correct.

Variation A is sort of "Purdie-ized," with all the ghosts written in. Variation B is a written example of the technique I talked about on the DVD of playing in groups of 4 in a triplet pattern. You can see the 4 grouping underneath to highlight where they fall. It's a cool way to make the groove seem like it's falling off a cliff, just for second.

Groove 97 Track 69

ODD METERS

Variation A

Variation B

CHART

The advanced 7 is going to take you on full-throttle wild ride. There is so much going on with this piece of music that you're going to go nuts figuring it all out. In a good way! It's nice that the main groove isn't difficult to play, even though the tempo is scooting along at a nice clip. The first half of variation A is built on a simple paradiddle that sounds very cool. Variation B is what it would look like if you extended the basic ride pattern to flow over the barline, making it a 2-bar phrase.

Inside this song, you'll find a half-time *feel* at the top (rather than pure half-time, which would actually halve the tempo), as well as unison lines and a great solo section over a four-bar vamp. It's all happening fast, and you need to be able to shift between grooves and unison lines seamlessly. Do not play this track if you can't play the others with confidence and clarity. Playing hard things poorly is a waste of time.

ODD METERS
Groove 98 Track 70

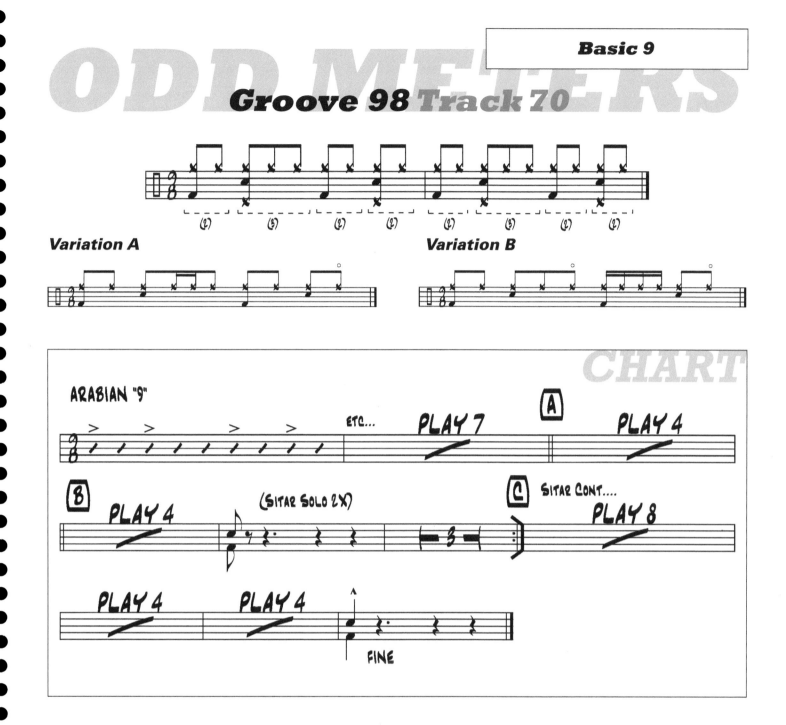

Variation A

Variation B

CHART

ARABIAN "9"

ETC... PLAY 7

[A] PLAY 4

[B] PLAY 4

(SITAR SOLO 2X)

[C] SITAR CONT.... PLAY 8

PLAY 4

PLAY 4

FINE

We've arrived at the "breakthrough" odd-meter: 9. Now we're dealing with four subgroups, and if you can function comfortably these four groups, you can usually just start to chain groups together as much as you need. The counting for our basic 9 is slightly different from the other basic grooves, where the 3 was on the end of the chain. Now, our counting pattern will be 2-3-2-2, counted exactly like this: 1-2-1-2-3-1-2-1-2.

The musicians wound up (through no coaching from me) giving this an interesting global flavor. When we were coming up, we all played gigs like weddings, and the coolest weddings were always when the families came from some culturally interesting place like India, Morocco, or Turkey. They'd often have two bands. One would play the music of their homeland, and we'd play everything else. What a great learning experience hearing these incredible musicians play the real music! *(Never let anyone tell you playing a gig like a wedding is not cool or whatever. There are opportunities to learn on every gig, I don't care what it is. The smart musicians take every opportunity they can to play and learn. And you're getting paid! What's not to love?)*

All the same rules apply to this basic groove. You may have trouble in the beginning with this longer chain. So what? Keep at it. Practice with the bonus track that features a vocal running through the song. It will help, trust me. The musicians are hammering out the pattern clearly, and you'll catch on in no time. Hear the Sitar pattern staying exactly on the counting?

ODD METERS
Groove 99 Track 71

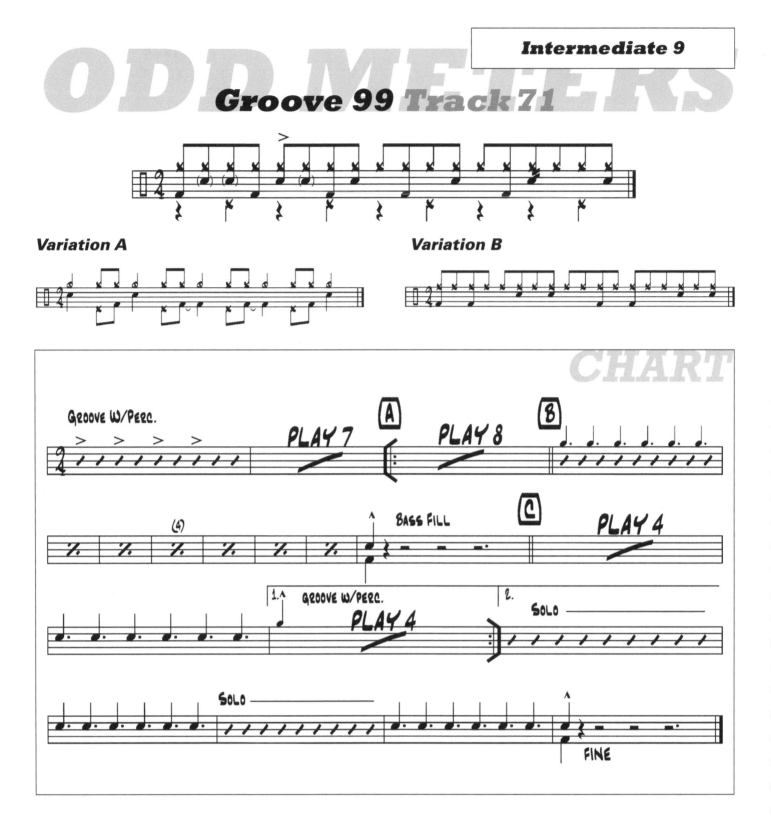

Variation A

Variation B

CHART

Here's a groove written to intentionally flow across across the groups (2-2-2-3), so the drumming isn't marking the 1s of each subgroup so bluntly. In fact, the bass drum doesn't play on any 1s at all except the first downbeat of each measure, creating a feeling of one long bar of 9.

The time signature is 9/4, and man, that is an impressively long bar, isn't it? I talk about the groove construction on the DVD—the buzz on beat 8, and how the hi-hat kicks off the groove on beat 9, etc.—so I won't go through it again here. Letter B has a great compositional feature where the entire band shifts the grouping and plays dotted quarters, so that section can be counted in 3 groups of 3 (1-2-3-1-2-3-1-2-3).

Variation A and B offer up different concepts. Variation A has a half-time ride pattern that you could continue over the bar line as long as you like. Variation B has a bass drum/snare drum pattern in 5/8 inside the 9/4. See it? Try it! You can keep the 5/8 pattern going as long as you want, to create a real skewing of the groove—but don't lose where 1 is. Oh, other musicians don't like that. No, really, they don't.

ODD METERS
Groove 100 Track 72

Variation A

Variation B

I played this groove and asked the band where the groupings were, and three great musicians gave me three different answers. Perfect! That's exactly what I wanted. Groove 100 is a groove that you can count several ways, and each way is valid. The way I conceived of it, and the way I wrote it in the book and on the poster, is 2-2-3-2. But you can also think of it as 2-2-2-3, or even 3-3-3 (especially on the B sections).

The track speaks for itself; you'll have your hands full for quite awhile. This track is a beast, and you should feel no pressure to play it if you aren't ready. But if you are, go for it! Have a great time, close the door, make mistakes, and let your imagination go wild on this piece of music.

Chapter 7

GLOBAL TOURS

Global Tour #5

Groove Essentials is all about solidifying our foundation to prepare for real-life musical events. For professionals using *GE*—and for those who aspire to be professionals—the epic adventures of the Global Tours is where it all comes together: the grooves, fills, time signatures, pockets, ghosts/grace notes, dynamics, reading, and (of course) the transitional elements required when segueing from one tune to another.

As you already know, the Global Tours are my attempt to recreate the mix tapes I used to make for my own practice *(cassettes back in the day—they used to jam and you'd have to use a pencil to spin them out. Made ya tough…)*. Each Global Tour is a multi-part adventure usually spanning about fifteen minutes in length, with no stops and at least four rude and musically cruel transitions. These Global Tours are trickier than in the original book, requiring extremely clever drumming to have the transitions make any kind of musical sense at all. And, as usual, it's usually you making the transition from one tempo and feel to the other—setting up the new tempo and groove for the entire band. No pressure…

Here are the grooves in Global Tour #5

- **Fast Rock**
- **Slow Partido Alto**
- **Fast Funk**
- **Slow Rock Blues 12/8 shuffle thing**
- **Fast Ridless Swing**

Transitional Points:

You've only got four beats to set up letter B, with a solo that not only introduces a new tempo but also connects two drastically different feels.

The four-bar solo into letter C has a completely new transitional element: an accelerating (accelerando) solo. Not all tempo transitions are static. Some, like this one, are moving targets. Listen to—and bury—the click.

While we accelerated during our solo, the piano player has to slow down (decelerando) into letter F. He only settles in about two beats before the groove, so you have to listen—and listen hard.

You hear about sightings of "metric modulations" thrown around all the time (often incorrectly, to describe simple syncopations), but here is a real live one in the wild. The quarter-note triplet becomes the dotted 8th two bars before G. It's not as bad as it sounds the first time you hear it. Well, okay, it probably is, but that's the fun!

Global Tour #6

On the menu today:

- (really) Fast Rock Shuffle
- Slow "four on the snare" Rock
- Medium 5/4 Groove
- (very) Slow Rock Ballad
- Fast 6/8 Half-time Afro-Rock Fusion

Transitional Points:

Again, you only have four little beats—just four little beats—to bring the whole band to a soft yet confident landing into letter C.

Ten bars before letter E (don't forget that 7x repeat counts as seven bars), you have to jump up the tempo and switch your brain, ears, and mind over to 5/4—all while you play a two-bar solo that sets up the band. No problem. Is there anything else they might like us to do? Wash their cars, pick up their dry cleaning? Jeez…

You're going to love this one, and I'm putting it in because I've seen it before. You'll thank me if it ever happens to you. Two bars before H: Read it and laugh. Done? Good, 'cuz it ain't a joke. A 15-second drum solo. That's right, 15 seconds. I did an industrial gig (basically a corporate gig that can feature anything and everything), and there was a scene change that just needed "A Flurry of Sound!" Well, I guess I looked "flurry" because the music director asked me to insert a loud 15-second open drum solo. Oh, and also to wind it down at the end to hear the click and bring everyone into the next section. Not very musically satisfying (to say the least), but sometimes you have to do what you have to do. So, play a solo and wind it down while listening for the click to set up the next tempo. It's a lot harder than it sounds. Well, actually it does sound kind of hard.

And finally, at letter I, there's an instantly-occurring, ice-cold tempo change and time signature shift. You really have to be ready BEFORE you get to the transition, or you'll never get it. If the wheels come off the bus on abrupt solos like this, they almost never get back on. Stay alert.

GLOBAL TOURS

Global Tour #7

And finally, a global tour that will keep you up at night, in a good way I hope. Here we go:

- Fast 5/8
- Medium 9/4
- Fast 7/8
- Slow Swing Funk
- (Very, Very) Fast Latin

You know what to look for in the transitions by now, and these are especially challenging. Remember: Perseverance is key, because this is a tough piece of music. Don't give up!

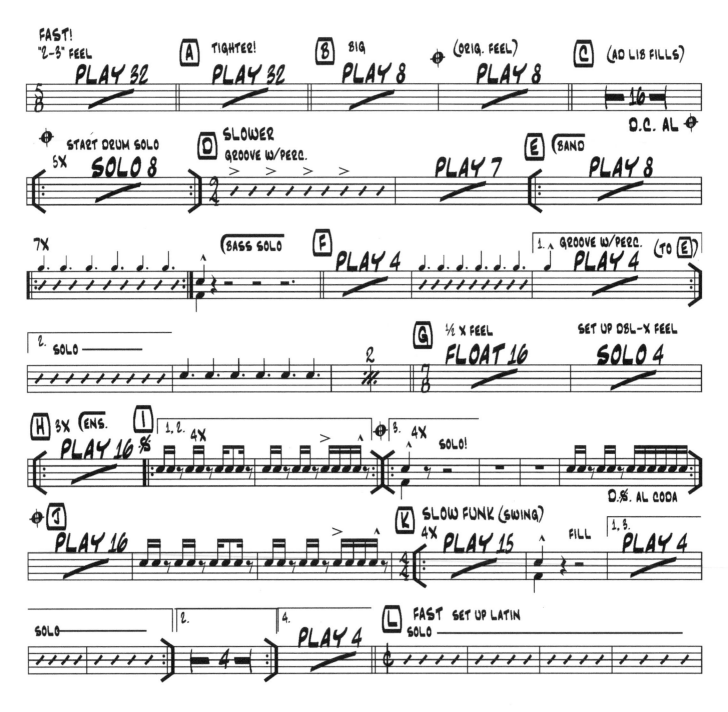

Global Tour #8
An Orchestral Experience for Drummers

In the original *GE*, the final Global Tour was a piece of original music called "Endure" that I wrote for my appearance at the 2002 Modern Drummer Festival. Because of its difficulty, there was some internal debate as to its inclusion in the package, but judging from the reaction, we made the correct choice. "Endure" has been used by students as a solo feature, an audition piece, and as a YouTube favorite to showcase their own fantastic interpretations. Obviously, you guys like the hard stuff. (Me too!) So, in the spirit of giving you something different and challenging, I'm very excited to unveil this piece of music. I believe we're going to offer up something for drummers never seen before in any educational package.

My motivation for arranging this piece is the regret I see time and again from the drummers who quit their school music program and now realized with they missed. That's why I'm such a vocal advocate of joining your school band, no matter how good or bad it may be. If you don't think playing in a school orchestra will make you a stronger groove player and a better musician, put this book down now and take up gardening. I'm not kidding.

If you are a serious student of drums, you may be thinking about gigs, and how to get more of them. Well, orchestras often hire drumset "specialists" to play specific pieces of music, and I've been called to play gigs as diverse as backing up the legendary Canadian Brass, or playing the drumset part on "Symphonic Dances" from *West Side Story*. While I surely can't give you decades of orchestral training in one piece of music, I believe that this will be an exciting introduction for drummers who crave this type of classical music experience. It's challenging, chaotic, and really, really fun.

I could write a full chapter on this piece alone, but there are five major concepts to absorb that are unique to this composition:

1. **Orchestral "time" is different from modern rhythm-section time. It breathes and flows and is subject to many different interpretations—even if it is supposedly steady. There are tempo changes all over this monster. Be ready for them.**
2. **The chart has specific written parts to play, but also a lot of "ad-lib" sections. Know the difference.**
3. **You must count rests! While there are some rests in *GE*, you are playing the majority of the time. In concert percussion literature, you rest the majority of time, and counting rests is a huge part of the gig.**
4. **Understand the crucial concept that the word "groove" means different things to different ensembles! While orchestras don't "groove" like we, as drummers, are used to, they do have a unique feel and can be surgically precise in their own way.**
5. **While I said previously that reading isn't necessary to use *Groove Essentials*, on this piece it is. You simply can't get orchestral gigs like this if you can't read, and that's just the truth. So, if you can't read well (or even at all), I hope this inspires you to get those reading chops together. I'll have something to help soon…**

You'll find two versions of this global tour on your disc. One version has me playing the drums, and the other has no drums with a little click to help with the transitions. Notice the chart is hand-written (by yours truly) in my supremely mediocre manuscript. Hand-written charts are very common, and compared to some, mine looks like a Picasso! The advanced students among you should write **your own chart** with **your own drumset arrangement**. Force yourself to write a completely different drumset part than mine (there are many possibilities). And, while your chart doesn't have to be gorgeous, it does have to be readable. The percussion potential on this arrangement is limited only by your imagination. So, as you strive for performance excellence, remember to take chances and push yourself outside your comfort zone. That's where the good stuff is…

Global Tour #8 Track 76

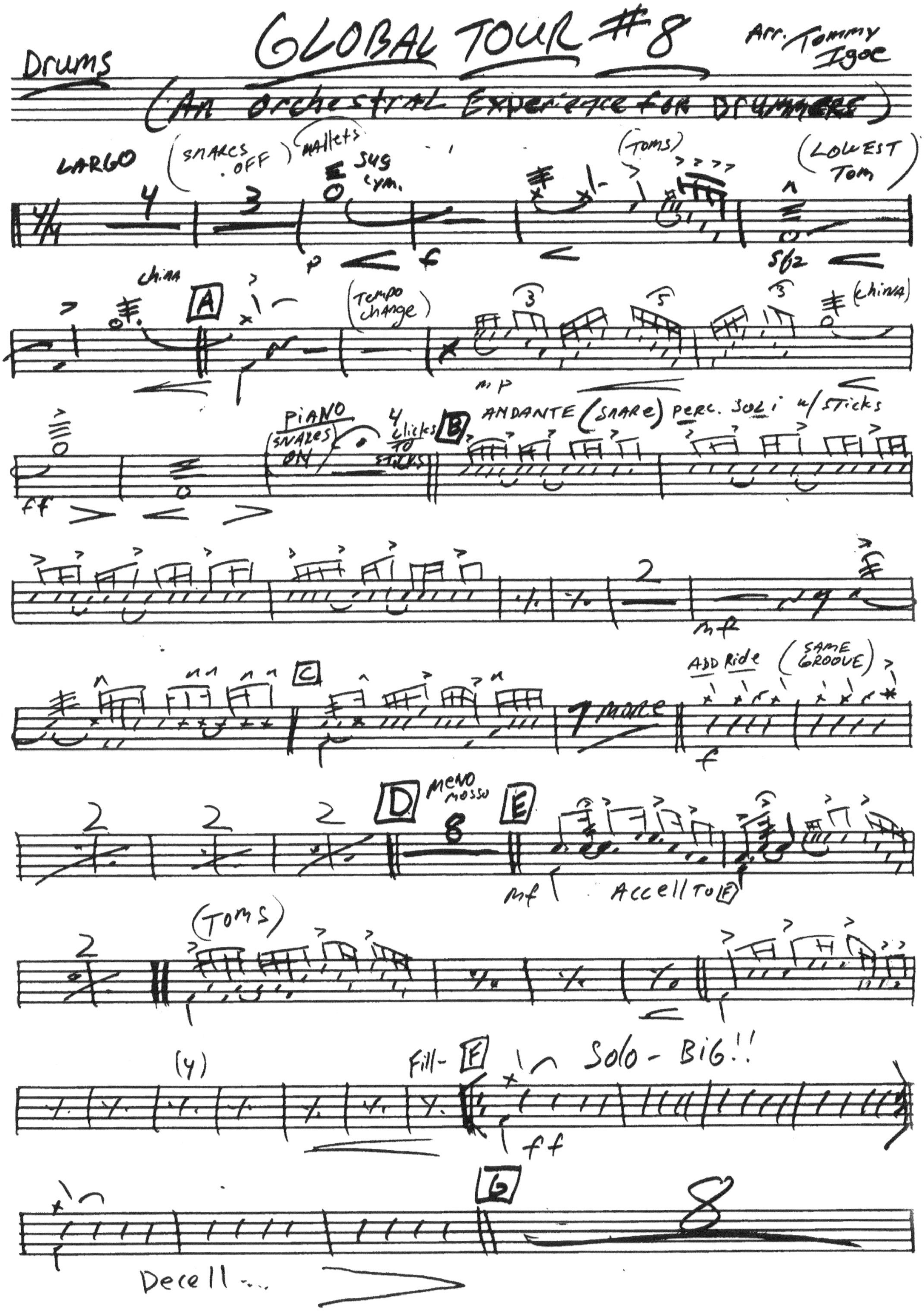

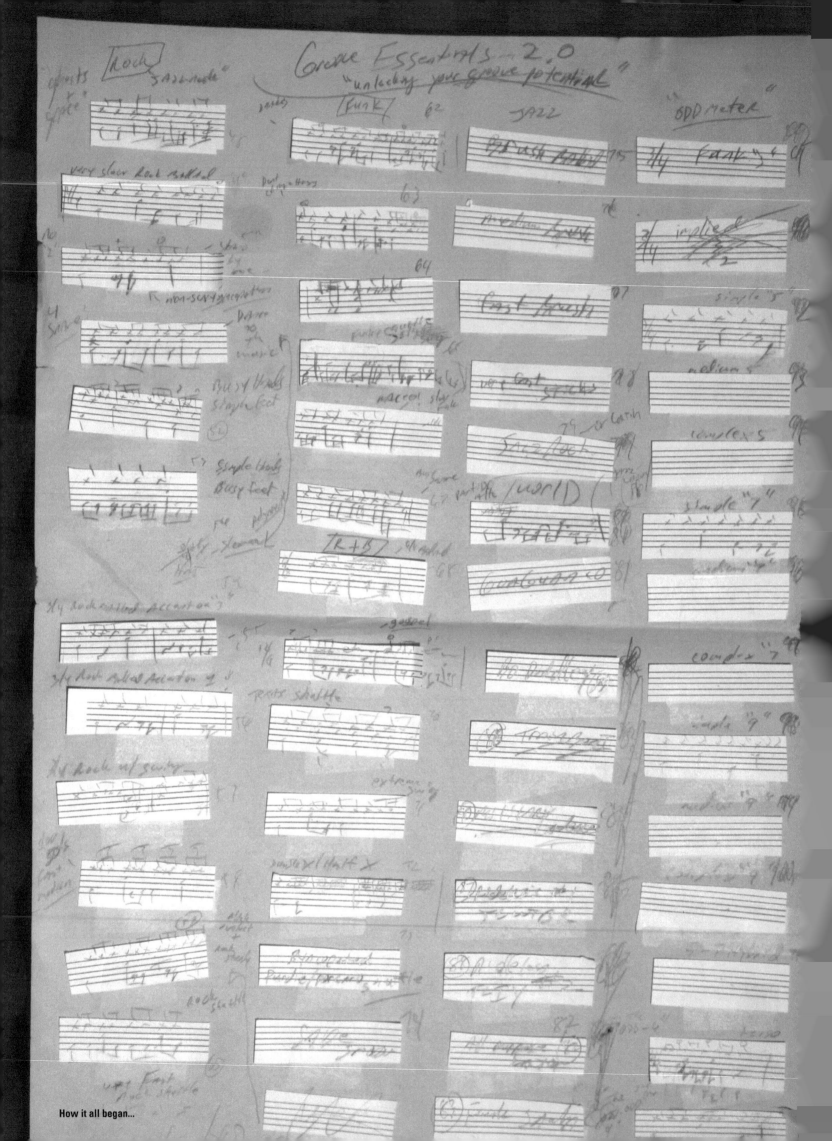

How it all began...

The Journey Never Ends...

100 grooves, 8 global tours, and nearly 190 play-along tracks later, here we are. We've spent so much time together, you and I, that we should really think about going steady. It's hard to say goodbye after everything we've been through but, as I've said, these books aren't designed to last you a month or a year, but forever. For as long as you play drums, *GE* will be here waiting for you.

Remember— *GE* is designed for you to fail on your first attempt. Why? Because a book you play well the first time is a waste of money. A good book, as I said before, is like a friendly sparring partner that occasionally gets a good shot in. So when you get to a full-bar solo and there is no click to keep time, you'll soon discover just how solid your personal command of time is. Most importantly, you'll discover your tendencies. Do you rush that solo or drag? If you play it 10 times, how many solos are rushed? Dragged? Spot-on perfect? Observe your own personal tendencies (we all have them) and acknowledge them as part of who you are as a musician. That is how you gain musical control over your tendencies; you must first acknowledge that they are there in the first place.

I received so many interesting questions as we came up to the end of the *GE 2.0* project that I thought many people would enjoy seeing what is on the minds of other *GE* users. Here are a few in no particular order:

Q: Should I wait until I have a song perfect before I go on to the next song in *GE*?

A: What is perfect? I don't think it exists, so you'll be on Groove 1 Slow forever! No, it doesn't have to be perfect. Just stay on it until you feel pretty good about it. Then, most importantly, come back to it later.

Q: I just don't like jazz. I want to, but I don't like it. I'm 16 and it just sounds like noise to me. Help!

A: Ahh!—A common predicament. I suggest starting out with something that has a groove that your ear is used to. Spyro Gyra, Fourplay, and YellowJackets are a few bands that I bet you'll enjoy, and they are great musicians (no matter what the jazz police say). After that, listen to some contemporary big bands, like The Big Phat Band, or my own Birdland Big Band. If you enjoy that, listen to some Buddy Rich and Count Basie to get a sense of history. From that point, I suggest listening to Cannonball Adderley for your first small group experience, which will open you up to all the other great jazz music that awaits. It's all about easing your ear into the genre.

Q: How long did it take to write the *GE* books?

A: The first book took about a year. *GE 2.0* took over 2 years.

Q: I can't read. I've tried but I don't like it at all and just can't get it.

A: Yes, you can! I'll be addressing this shortly, with a unique solution for you and everyone else who "just can't read." Remove the word "can't" from your vocabulary. I know you can do it.

Q: How often do you practice?

A: Not often enough. That's why I tell my young students to practice as much as you can now, because if your career takes off, your practice opportunities plunge, unfortunately.

Q: The World grooves are so cool! But I'm terrible at them. What should I do?

A: Remember, you have to listen to Brazilian music to sound good at Brazilian music, and so on. Listen, and more importantly, play along with some of the CDs I recommend in the first book. You'll get it. My samba was so horrible at first—sounded like a flat tire. Keep at it!

Q: I see World grooves of the same name notated differently. Who's wrong?

A: Why does someone have to be wrong? I took lessons from several Latin masters and they contradicted each other constantly. That's okay, one wasn't right or wrong; I just learned different ways to play grooves and then apply them as I see fit. World grooves can have many "right" ways. Don't let it stress you out. Keep an open mind and stay receptive to new ideas.

Q: I want to play on Broadway like you do. How do I take lessons for that?

A: With all due respect to Broadway musicians, I really wouldn't *try* to be a Broadway musician. Just study to be the best musician you can be, period. Learn styles, genres and history, then you'll be prepared for any gig that comes your way, including a Broadway show where you might have to play many styles. But you need experience interpreting a conductor, which is why I'm such an advocate for joining your local school music program. Out of school? Then go join a community orchestra. Even if they don't let you play, just watch them rehearse! See what a conductor looks like. Do whatever it takes to get that experience.

Q: What's the one thing I can do to make me a better drummer?

A: Take piano lessons. I'm not kidding.

Q: I got run off a jam session the other day. The bass player hated me. I just want to quit.

A: Don't worry, we've all got a story like that. Do not quit, just be honest with yourself. Look, jam sessions are the musicians' equivalent of recess. It's where everybody's personalities really come out, and the class bullies run the show. So you met a nasty bass player. There are a ton of them, as well as nasty drummers, pianists, vocalists, etc. Is there a musical reason he didn't like you? Be honest with yourself and don't let emotion skew your assessment of what happened. Everyone has bad moments. Evvvvereeeeeonnnne! Learn and move on.

Q: I saw you at Birdland with your band and I was shocked by the speed and power. Um, why don't you play like that on the GE dvd?

A: Am I that bad on the DVD? Kidding—I know what you mean. I don't play like you heard me at Birdland because that's not what *GE* is about. I wanted to invite *everyone* in with my playing on the DVD, not scare them off. Also, it would have been inappropriate for me to play anything more on this groove-oriented material. What kind of example would I be setting? I told the publishers to throw stuff at me if I overplayed—and they did, too. They enjoyed it a little too much, if you ask me.

Francisco Paz, helping Tommy remember what groove to play.

A Page for Educators

One of the most gratifying things about the reaction to *GE* was the fact that so many educators are using it with their students. Of course, a drummer can just buy the book and work on it alone, but the material really comes alive with a good teacher to listen, coach, discuss, and polish your performances.

I was informed some clever teachers are using the DVD (on a laptop) to play my demonstration for their student. Then, the teacher and student work through the groove together with a metronome or however they like. It's like a three-person team in the room. Then, if the student is ready, they try one of the songs. They watch me play the short version on the DVD, and then the student tries the play-along right there. Next, the teacher can demonstrate some stuff themselves, replay my demo, or whatever they like. It's a very exciting use of the DVD that I thought was brilliant. Why didn't I think of that?

Of course, by far the best part of *GE* is to use the tracks to record your students. Any simple and inexpensive recording solution will work. Just go to your local music store (that has a technology department), and you'll find many appropriate products that can transform your teaching experience into something on another level completely. Too many educators are stuck with last century's tools (Jeez, my Dad was recording his students with a Revox reel-to-reel in the 1970s! No excuses…). Start recording your students with the *GE* material and you'll not only notice your students' satisfaction go through the roof, I'll bet you'll get more students, too.

I also suggest letting students play uninterrupted for the entire length of the play-along and then, instead of you telling them what happened, have them tell you. Ask them questions like:

Can you sing the bass line?
Why did you play a fill at bar 7?
What is musically different at letter C?
Describe the guitar part to me. Is it clean or dirty?
Is the band softer or louder on the second time through the form?
Is the bass in front of or behind the guitar, and what are you going to do about it?

And so on. Asking questions makes students think about and justify their musical decisions. With the *GE* material, they are forced to make decisions on their own, because the chart doesn't tell them what to do except in the broadest of senses. A verbal dialogue about a musical performance that just happened is one of the best techniques that you can employ to reach into a student's musical mind and help coach them to a higher level.

And to all you full-time teachers out there: you have my undying respect. Teaching, as my father used to say, is a "tough buck." Private drum teachers are the front-line soldiers of the drumming arts, and I'm one of the guys who know it. So here's a big "thank you" for dedicating your talents to teaching the art of drumming at the highest levels possible.

Thanks to the Team

As I said in the original *GE*, you can't possibly produce a work of this monstrous size on your own. I had a lot of help, and all are the best in the biz at what they do. Thanks:

Jo Hay for the brilliant design once again.

Joe Bergamini for the deft and clever editing, making it look like I know how to write, which is no small feat, I'll tell ya! *(Tommy, this last word should be "you" as "ya" is not technically a w…) It's alright Joe, we're done…*

Jack Mansager for engraving mastery. Jack really is a wonder (look at all this notation). But, you know, I did write it all by hand first, and that was hard. I got cramps and stuff. Hey Jack, give me some of that money!

The Army of Proofreaders: **Brendan Buckley, Joe Choroszewski, Wayne Dunton, Lee Jeffryes, Carter McLean,** and **Tom Nichols**. Did you know the first *Groove Essentials* had basically no errors in it? A herculean feat when publishing a book this complicated. Well, that's because of these guys. Let's all hope they did as well this time. Let's meet back in a year or so, and we'll know. I'm holding their checks until then. Ha! That's funny. What checks?

Francisco Paz, my assistant and tech, for his untiring work and great spirit. Where's my phone?!

My friends and publishers, **Rob Wallis** and **Paul Siegel** of Hudson Music, who are the best at what they do—can anyone tell me what that is, exactly? Anyone, anyone?—and have the belief that I'm only partially insane when I tell them my ideas. Wait until they hear what's next! *Bwah ha ha…!*

The *Groove Essentials* band (L to R): Kevin Kuhn, Tommy, Vashon Johnson, Ted Baker

Tommy, asking the booth for one more take.

Allen Farnham

My personal gratitude to my indescribably supportive family, who haven't seen much of me for the final four months of production, as everything came to it's frenzied climax.

And lastly the amazing musicians of *Groove Essentials:*
Ted Baker: Keyboards
Vashon Johnson: Basses
Kevin Kuhn: Guitars
Allen Farnham: Piano
Rolando Morales-Matos: Percussion

Without them, *Groove Essentials* is just a book—just notes on a page. Why *GE* gets the attention it gets is because of the music. These guys are geniuses. We recorded 74 original pieces of music in three 14-hour days of recording. That… is… nuts! I didn't even have to trick them this time. They actually came willingly, knowing the pounding they were going to get. Go figure. But holy moly, did the studio smell nasty by day three. Pizza, popcorn, beer, fast food, candy, pretzels, nuts, four sweaty musicians, and a closed soundproofed room with no windows. A bad olfactory combination, but ahhhh—sweet, sweet music, baby!

Thanks also to Vic Firth sticks, Evans drumheads, Drum Workshop drums, Zildjian cymbals, Latin Percussion, and Rhythm Tech—the best companies any artist could want to work with, making the best gear any drummer could want to play.

Glenn Banning and Tommy review the master groove chart.

The crew, playing "Rock Band" on a break.

Paul Siegal and Rob Wallis of Hudson Music, with Tommy.

Rolando Morales-Matos

BIOGRAPHY

Tommy Igoe has been at the forefront of drumset performance and education for the last 25 years. He was drumming before he could walk and has never stopped. During his high school years, he played drums at every opportunity while simultaneously studying piano and performing with the Bayonne Bridgemen.

At the age of 18, he embarked on his first global tour and from that point his career took off. The next 15 years saw Tommy performing with everyone from Lauryn Hill to Art Garfunkel, with many more in between. He also started his educational contributions, teaching privately and in select universities. His unique and realistic methodology soon made him one of the most sought after private teachers in the country.

In 1997, Tommy wrote the drumset book for *The Lion King* in what would be a groundbreaking theatrical event. More than 10 *Lion King* companies in 8 different countries are currently performing Tommy's drumset book. Presently, he serves as principal drummer and assistant conductor with the original company on Broadway.

In 2002, Tommy joined with Hudson Music to bring his teaching philosophies to DVD, starting with the global best-seller, *Getting Started On Drums,* followed shortly thereafter by the original and groundbreaking *Groove Essentials*. He currently is the leader of the most popular weekly jazz event in New York, with the *Birdland Big Band* at the legendary Birdland jazz club. Visit tommyigoe.com for more about Tommy and his music.

Tommy Igoe plays Vic Firth sticks and mallets, Zildjian cymbals, D.W. drums, Evans drumheads, L.P. percussion and Rhythm Tech accessories exclusively.

Tommy soloing at Musikmesse in Frankfurt, Germany.